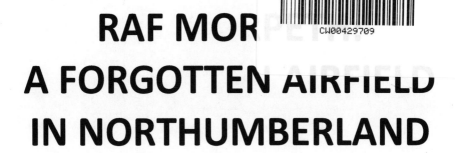

RAF MOR
A FORGOTTEN AIRFIELD
IN NORTHUMBERLAND

GRAEME RENDALL

Reiver Country Books
(in conjunction with Amazon)

Also by the same author:

To the Ends of the Earth: A Snapshot of Aviation in North-Eastern Siberia, Summer 1992 (published in eBook and softback formats)

UFOs Before Roswell: European Foo-Fighters 1940-1945
(published in eBook, softback and hardback formats)

Northumberland Aviation Stories
(published in eBook, softback and hardback formats)

Northumberland Aviation Stories: Volume Two
(published in eBook, softback and hardback formats)

Shadows Over The Reich: More European Foo-Fighter Tales
(forthcoming, due for publication in late 2022)

Fireballs Over The Pacific: Far Eastern Foo-Fighters 1941-1945
(forthcoming, due for publication in early 2023)

CONTENTS

INTRODUCTION

The locked gate on the western side of the aerodrome, which leads to the foundations of two of the three original T1 hangars at RAF Morpeth. The metal barrier behind the gate carries a warning: "MOD Land – No Parking At Gate – 24 Hour Access". A public footpath runs along the old road, but access is via a kissing gate about twenty yards off to the left of shot. This gate is opened for Sunday car boot sales and other occasional events on the old aerodrome. (Author)

What remains of the former Royal Air Force aerodrome near Morpeth, some fifteen miles north of Newcastle-upon-Tyne, lies not far north of the present-day Newcastle International Airport. Whilst standing at a farm gate on the side of the Saltwick-Mitford road, 400 yards south of the Tranwell Woods road junction, and then looking westwards over the field in front of you, it is possible to look across the site of the three former runways and also some of the eastern perimeter track and old hard-standings. This farm gate is not too far from the spot where a Westland Lysander target tug aircraft overturned on landing and completely blocked the road on one June afternoon in 1942. On the eastern side of the road, located next to the trees, there is a large brick structure, another relic from the brief period of time during World War Two when this quiet corner of Northumberland reverberated to the sound of aircraft engines.

RAF Morpeth was never a front-line aerodrome, engaged in the air defence of Newcastle or the port of Blyth, nor did it house bomber squadrons that took the fight directly to Nazi Germany. Instead, it remained a backwater in terms of operational flying, but quiet it was not. The RAF training unit based there was constantly churning out qualified air gunners that were in great demand to man the defensive stations in Bomber Command's Wellington, Stirling, Lancaster, and Halifax aircraft. Coastal Command also needed gunners for its Sunderland, Catalina, and Liberator patrol aircraft that flew long, monotonous sorties over the North Atlantic, looking for U-boats. Whilst it may not have been a sought-after posting for instructors, pilots or officers, the Air Gunners School at Morpeth was certainly an important one, and the work that was carried out there in teaching the constant influx of trainee gunners proved invaluable to the overall war effort.

Morpeth, like most other RAF stations during World War Two, was also one where personnel from many countries around the world served, especially those who had to flee Poland from the clutches of the Nazis. Indeed, Polish airmen made up a large proportion of the pilots at Morpeth. Unfortunately, due to the changing political climate in eastern Europe, many of them never returned home after it was all over, and an even smaller number never left Morpeth at all, as their bodies were buried in a churchyard located in the town.

You will not find much of RAF Morpeth's wartime history in books covering the aerial history of World War Two. Virtually nothing about what Morpeth was used for afterwards has been listed anywhere else. Seventeen pages of a rather good book about Northumberland's airfields are devoted to Morpeth and that has been the best summary available of the aerodrome's history until now. Similarly, there is also a dearth of photographs taken there during the war that have been reproduced elsewhere, either in books or online. Ordinary servicemen and women were largely forbidden from having cameras whilst on duty and taking photographs on the aerodrome would have attracted unwelcome attention. However, some official pictures were presumably taken at the time, although they have proved surprisingly difficult to track down. This particular account has been compiled from a number of sources, including The National Archives and people who visited the site during the war as Air Cadets or as civilians who lived locally.

This curious-shaped structure (looking like a flattened oval, built from pre-cast concrete sections) can be found near to the surviving Miskins blister hangar, close to the current northern boundary fence. It is a "Motley Stalk" anti-aircraft gun position for a single machine-gun, fitted onto a tripod. The concrete walls would have offered some protection from bomb blast, but not much. The exact site of this structure can easily be located due to the large tree growing from within the ring! (Author)

This paperback edition includes much more content than the eBook version that was published in August 2021. Since then I have come into possession of a lot more information about the old aerodrome, and therefore could not simply withhold it from readers. A new version of the eBook will also be made available.

Members of the Morpeth History Matters Facebook group also provided me with invaluable assistance. At the time of writing, there were no signboards or wartime trails around the former RAF Morpeth site to tell people what happened there. Hopefully, this book will therefore help those who are interested in learning more about what happened at the station. It is a story worth telling, if not simply to shed light on a forgotten yet vitally important aspect of air operations during World War Two. If you have enjoyed this history of RAF Morpeth, please leave a review of the book at Amazon.co.uk. It will be appreciated.

You can reach me on Twitter: @Borders750, or via email at: reivercountrybooks@gmail.com

Graeme Rendall
Northumberland,
August 2021.

AN AERODROME IS BORN

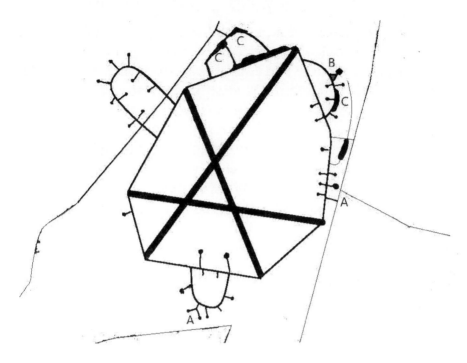

A plan of Morpeth aerodrome in 1944. The three main runways are linked by a perimeter track which also connects to a series of "frying pan" type aircraft hard-standings, some of which are situated off their own taxiway "loops". The letters signify the locations of gun firing butts (A), the Miskins Blister Hangar that still survives today (B) and the locations of the three T1 "shed" type hangars (C) which have all been dismantled and removed. The roads on either side of the old aerodrome site are also shown, as is the old road (now a public footpath) which led eastwards to the RAF Stannington site, where the School of Accounting was based. The line along the bottom of the plan is today a footpath and gives a good view of one of the butts. (Plan drawn by the author, based on aerial images and wartime plans provided by RAF Museum)

In 1941, after the Battle of Britain and Night Blitz had ended, the RAF moved into a new phase of the war. This involved taking the fight to the enemy's homeland, which at the time seemed to be the only effective measure of attacking Germany since their armies appeared to be increasingly victorious on all land fronts. Bomber Command was in the vanguard of this effort, with its strategic bomber force in the early throes of developing into a successful means of disrupting and destroying the enemy's capacity to fight effectively. The town of Morpeth, in southern Northumberland, had not been immune to the Blitz itself: bombs had been dropped in the vicinity by raiders on occasions, most of them jettisoned by lost or damaged aircraft seeking to lighten their loads for the return trip to bases in Occupied Europe. In addition, the enemy had arrived more directly. In May 1941, a *Luftwaffe* Heinkel He 111 bomber bound for Glasgow was shot down by an Acklington-based night-fighter and had come down in Bluebell Woods, just to the north-east of the town itself. The five-man crew survived and were taken prisoner.

Plans had already been in hand since 1940 to introduce new, larger four-engined heavy bomber types that could drop worthwhile amounts of bombs on Nazi industry and infrastructure. A huge increase in the number of aircrew was needed for these new, larger, more sophisticated bombers, and qualified gunners would be required to man their turrets. In the case of the Stirling, Halifax and Lancaster, a mid-upper turret was fitted in addition to nose and tail turrets. This meant a sixth and often seventh crew member was needed, as the ageing Whitley, Hampden and Wellingtons already in service only had crews of four or five.

The existing gunnery training set-up was judged inadequate to cope with the planned increase in the numbers of airmen, so it was decided to create a group of new units, the Air Gunners Schools. These would have to be situated away from the south of England, where space for aerodromes was at a premium and there was an ever-present threat of attack from the *Luftwaffe*. In late 1940, a whole host of new aerodrome sites were examined, situated right across northern England and southern Scotland. Locations which had previously been used as First World War landing grounds were considered ideal for development into new aerodromes, and the one just south of Morpeth town centre was not overlooked by the planners in the Air Ministry.

The former landing site at Stannington Station, used infrequently by Airco DH.4 and DH.9 light bombers belonging to No.52 Training Depot Station at Cramlington, was looked at by the men from the Ministry. These aircraft had occasionally flown from this grass field in 1918 and it is believed that Cobham's Tours and other "flying circus" type companies may have operated from the old site during the 1920s and early 1930s. However, the old landing ground was soon rejected, possibly because the site itself, situated just south of Stannington Station, between the Great North Road and the main Newcastle to Edinburgh railway line, was unable to offer enough space in which to construct modern runways.

The approximate location of the WW1 Stannington Landing Ground, situated between the East Coast railway line and the Great North Road, just south of Stannington Station. The site was deemed too restrictive to use when the Air Ministry were looking for suitable aerodrome sites in 1940. I took this image from a southbound train on 16th September 2021. (Author)

Another location, just a mile-and-a-half or so to the west, was therefore chosen for the site of the new Morpeth aerodrome. The plans were quickly approved, with appropriate orders being given for building work to start as soon as possible. Construction of RAF Morpeth began in early 1941. The standard "triangle" pattern of three runways was laid down by John Laing of Carlisle, the company being responsible for building other airfields in Northumberland and Cumberland (as it was then known). Morpeth's three runways were laid out as follows: 05/23 at 1,400 yards in length, plus 11/29 and 17/35, both of which were 1,100 yards long. These were later extended to 1,800, 1,500 and 1,600 yards respectively. Each runway was 50 yards wide and constructed from tarmac. Unusually, two of the three runways at Morpeth intersected in a slight depression located in the middle of the planned site. This would cause no end of problems once training flights got underway in earnest.

Eventually, at least thirty-six circular hard-standings, each one of them some fifty feet in diameter, were built and linked to the perimeter track by short lengths of concrete taxiway. Each of these was large enough for a twin-engined aircraft to park on, and this prevented aircraft sinking into the soft grass if left for extended periods of time. Hard runways, perimeter tracks and parking areas were now standard for all new aerodromes although it had not always been so, since most sites at the start of the war were simply large grass fields, susceptible to the vagaries of the weather.

The official plans show that there were three T1 type hangars (also known as "sheds"), two situated in the north-western corner of the airfield and the third adjacent to the Saltwick to Mitford road, near the entrance to the flying field itself. The T1, built to Air Ministry drawing number 7541/41, was 90 feet wide and 175 feet long, with a clear door height of 19 feet. The "T" stood for "Temporary" or "Transportable", as they were intended to be moved around an aerodrome if required. The design was intended to be mass-produced, with interchangeable parts to allow rapid erection and dismantling if needed. At least one of the T1 hangars survived at Morpeth until the late 1980s before being dismantled.

The surviving Miskins Double Extra Over blister hangar at RAF Morpeth is located in the far north-eastern corner of the old aerodrome. It is used for agricultural storage. Structurally, it appears to be in reasonably good condition although end walls were added at some stage after World War Two as the building was originally open ended to allow up to two twin-engined Blackburn Botha aircraft to be stored inside. The public footpath crossing the northern side of the old station runs very close to this building as the photograph shows. This image was taken in March 2002. (Author)

In addition, Morpeth had a large number of smaller temporary hangars known as "blisters", due to the shape of their roofs. Three Miskins Extra Over and six Miskins Double Extra Over blisters were erected at Morpeth. The Extra Over had a span of 69 feet and was 20 feet high. With a length of 45 feet, it could accommodate a single Blackburn Botha or two Avro Ansons, although the latter would have been a tight squeeze. Most of these were sited just off the eastern perimeter track. Finally, there were also four Dorman Long Type blister hangars, three of which were situated on the large loop of taxiway beyond the lane running down the western edge of the aerodrome, and the fourth just off the main western perimeter track. Dorman Long Type blisters were slightly wider than the Miskins Extra Overs, so fitting a pair of Ansons would not have been too challenging. The plans also indicate that provision was made for a further eleven blisters, two off the western perimeter track and the others on the southern taxiway loop. Nine spaces are shown on the official plan, but no details are provided regarding the planned hangar types. However, a photo taken on 29th July 1942 shows five of the nine spaces being occupied by blister hangars, presumably Dorman Long or Miskins Over types.

The Miskins blister hangars were moved to different locations on the airfield during early 1944. An experiment, it was accomplished without dismantling the buildings! Although the T1 ("Transportable Shed") and "Enlarged Over Blister" hangars were designed to be transported from site to site, in practice it was unusual to see them moved once they were installed on an aerodrome, and therefore a film was made of the event. The Miskins Double Extra Over blister (designed to Air Ministry Works drawing no. 9392/42) was 91 feet wide and could accommodate a single twin-engined Blackburn Botha aircraft. It consisted of all-welded steel rib sections that were bolted together to form arches. Joined by steel ties and purlins of wood or steel, corrugated iron sheeting was used to cover them.

Buildings were built on both sides of the Saltwick to Mitford road. The bases on the aerodrome side of the road can still be seen today, including the motor transport sheds, the fuel compound, the squadron offices, and the gunnery flight offices. However, without a plan of the site, it is incredibly difficult to work out which is which.

The aerodrome eventually had two flight offices, one lying next to the Saltwick to Mitford road and the other near the present-day entrance from the Ponteland to Mitford road on the western side of the aerodrome, close to the offices of the towed target section. The original Watch Office (control tower), built to Air Ministry Drawing Number D046/40 and situated on its own on the aerodrome side of the eastern perimeter track, was replaced by an annex to the motor transport office. This was a Nissen hut located just east of the surviving Miskins blister hangar and close to the Saltwick to Mitford road, the annex serving as an improvised control tower. No.5007 Airfield Construction Squadron was responsible for carrying out this particular conversion job.

An old blast shelter lying inside Saltwick Plantation, the long strip of trees lying adjacent to the minor road running south from Tranwell Woods to Saltwick. The foundations of numerous buildings from the old Technical Site were still visible back in March 2002 when this photograph was taken. The trees and undergrowth have now all but hidden most of the remnants of the site, and given the amount of broken masonry, concrete and other rubble, together with ankle-breaking holes and other hazards lying deep in the ground vegetation, exploration is not recommended. However, there are a number of unofficial pathways through the plantation which are used by dog walkers living in the nearby St. Mary's Park estate. Some of them even follow the lines of the former roads through the old Technical Site, with sections of concrete being visible. (Author)

On the other side of the road, in the narrow strip of forest known as Saltwick Plantation, more buildings were located. This was the aerodrome's technical site, where the workshops, stores and armoury were situated. In addition, the parachute store and station offices, the latter housing the wireless telegraphy office, could be found in this area. A large aircraft marshalling area was also built next to the north-east side of the perimeter track, close to the present-day minor road from Saltwick to Mitford. This was to allow machines to carry out last-minute checks before taking-off without blocking either the taxiway or the runway. As intensive training was planned for Morpeth, it was incredibly important that everything ran smoothly, including the movement of aircraft around the aerodrome itself. "Traffic jams" when taking off or landing, coupled with pilots who chose the wrong taxiway or runway inevitably caused delays and occasionally accidents, some of them fatal. Delays on the aerodrome also translated into delays for the training courses, which of course had an adverse effect on the war effort.

One of the station's two machine-gun ranges, located just off the Tranwell Woods to Saltwick road at the southern end of Saltwick Plantation. The trainees would practice firing Browning machine-guns at the other side of this huge brick wall, sometimes from an old gun turret fixed onto a flatbed lorry. The public footpath here (visible right edge of image) used to be a road running from the Technical Site to nearby RAF Stannington. (Author)

One of the two machine gun ranges (built to Air Ministry Drawing Number 147/41) is located just east of the Saltwick-Mitford road. The second was built south of the southern taxiway loop and can still be seen from a farm gate at a sharp bend about half a mile south of the aerodrome. The southern taxiway loop itself disappeared during post-war quarrying work.

Apart from the two massive machine gun range structures, No.4 Air Gunners School, the unit which would move into Morpeth on its completion, had access to two Standard Free Gunnery Trainers, the first one being located in what is now the surviving Miskins blister hangar. The second was located within the instructional site. The gunnery trainer was a Frazer-Nash gun turret, mounted halfway up a tall metal framework, which was attached to a large hemispherical screen. The guns projected a graticule onto the screen, so the trainee knew what he was aiming at; the instructor stood on a platform above the turret and recorded the pupil's accuracy. Clouds could be simulated on the screen and special training films, with realistic targets such as Messerschmitt Bf 109s and Bf 110s, were also employed. Once trained on these synthetic devices, the pupils could move onto the Blackburn Bothas and Avro Ansons that were operated by the gunnery school. There were also two clay pigeon houses situated near the old watch office for less orthodox gunnery!

In addition to the aerodrome and the buildings immediately associated with it, RAF Morpeth also had a Communal Site, an Instructional Site, a Sick Quarters Site, two Women's Auxiliary Air Force (WAAF) sites and seven individually numbered sites for the other personnel based at the station. All of these sites were located in an arc from the north to the east of the aerodrome, the nearest (No.3 Site) being a couple of hundred yards away. The furthest was, not surprisingly, the Sewage Disposal and Waste Site, just to the south of Tranwell village. The following is a list of all of the dispersed sites, together with an idea of their individual functions:

Instructional Site: (located next to the present-day Woodside Cottage on the north side of the road running between the water tower and Tranwell Woods) This site included classrooms, a Link Trainer, the second Free Gunnery Trainer and two Turret Instruction buildings.

Communal Site: (located on the east side of the Tranwell-Stannington road, between the water tower and the Glororum junction). This site included messes, barracks, the senior officers' quarters, and the beer store!

Sick Quarters Site: (located on the west side of the Saltwick to Mitford road, between the main road and the Tranwell Woods junction. Fairly self-explanatory, this site included wards, an ambulance garage and the mortuary.

Sites No.1 through No.7 and the WAAF Sites:

No.1 (located to the east of the water tower and the Communal Site)

No.2 (located adjacent to Glororum, just north of the road west of the farm)

No.3 (located just east of the main aerodrome buildings, south of the "White House")

No.4 (located alongside the Tranwell-Stannington road just south of Tranwell)

No.5 (located just north of Well Hill on the West Side of the road)

No.6 (located just south of Well Hill on the West Side of the road)

No.7 (located southwest of the old Tranwell reservoirs)

All of these sites contained officers' quarters and airmen's barracks, apart from No.7 which just had the latter. Access to No.3 Site was via a road running past the entrance to No.5 Site, i.e., the opposite direction from the aerodrome itself.

The only surviving buildings of any size on the former WAAF Site No.1 at RAF Morpeth are the former Showers & Decontamination Block, together with its associated water tower. A Nissen hut was affixed to this end of the structure, as can be discerned by the curved wall ends. The "doorways" in the water tower were most likely the location of toilets, their actual doors having long since vanished. These buildings are in the middle of trees within privately owned land and access is normally prohibited due to safety issues. There are deep, water-filled holes within the trees which are very hard to spot due to the vegetation cover, so it is dangerous to explore further. I had permission from the landowner to visit this site. The image was taken in early August 2021. (Author)

<u>Women's Auxiliary Air Force Site No.1</u> (located opposite the Sick Quarters Site)

<u>WAAF Site No.2</u> (located north of WAAF Site No.1, near the main road to Whalton)

These sites had officers' and sergeants' quarters, plus airwomen's barracks. No.1 Site, which was also home to the WAAF Communal

Site, also housed a fuel compound and a hairdresser's room.

Sewerage Disposal and Waste Site (located just south of Tranwell village) This small area had tanks and filtration pools, a couple of small buildings and a blast shelter.

The construction of a proposed satellite aerodrome for the new station, which would have been located just outside the village of Longhirst, about three miles north-east of Morpeth town centre, was abandoned at the planning stage. The station therefore never did have its own relief landing ground, which would have allowed many more aircraft to operate at any one time. Concentrating all of the unit's machines at one aerodrome, with its intensive schedule of training flights, was essentially a recipe for disaster, and this was soon proved to be correct.

As the threat of German invasion had not yet gone away, the authorities arranged for timber barricades to be erected to obstruct the runways once they were completed, as the site was still not ready to accept the first RAF personnel. Given the enemy's success with surprise glider assaults at Eben Emael in May 1940 and the Corinth Canal in April 1941, it was considered wise to block the runways until the station was occupied. To defend against any possible German landings, an Army defence unit moved in on 29th September 1941. This small contingent of soldiers was led by Major A. S. C. Brown of the 12th Royal Lancers.

RAF Morpeth was built as a training station; one that would help to supply some of the large quantities of personnel required to take Bomber Command's planned bombing campaign directly to the *Reich*. An advance party of staff arrived at Morpeth in January 1942 but found that the facilities at the still incomplete aerodrome were quite primitive and that the local water supply was contaminated. Pilot Officer J. Middleton was among the group, posted to Morpeth "for defence duties", presumably as a liaison officer for the Army detachment. Weeks of organisation and hard labour were required to create a station fit for use by the staff and the trainees destined to receive tuition there.

Eventually, some 58 RAF officers, 153 non-commissioned officers and 1038 other ranks, plus 10 Women's Auxiliary Air Force officers, 427 WAAF NCOs and other ranks were eventually to serve at RAF Morpeth, together with the various trainees that would be posted there for varying periods of time. However, it would be some time before the station received its full complement of personnel.

On 31st January 1942, nearly three months before RAF Morpeth was ready to receive its first aircraft, a Hawker Hurricane fighter crash-landed in the southwest corner of the incomplete aerodrome. This was Mk.I V7613 from No.55 Operational Training Unit (OTU), based at RAF Usworth near Sunderland, which was flown by Pilot Officer Patterson, a Royal Canadian Air Force pilot. A bearing had seized in the engine, causing oil pressure to drop suddenly: the aircraft then caught fire, causing Patterson to crash land his Hurricane in the corner of the aerodrome The Canadian was uninjured, and the aircraft was later repaired; it served with No.288 Squadron before being finally struck from RAF charge in June 1944. The pilot appears to have survived the war, as his name is not listed on the Commonwealth War Graves Commission roll.

The first RAF personnel started to arrive in dribs and drabs over the winter, with the first motor transport (two lorries) appearing on 4th February 1942. By the 28th, enough bodies had turned up at the incomplete site in order to warrant the arrival of the station's first commanding officer, Wing Commander John Marson. He had joined the RAF as a cadet in 1924, becoming a pilot with No.13 Squadron two years later, and flying the Bristol F.2B Fighter. There, Marson took on the role of Armament Officer, something he would continue to carry out when he was transferred to No.30 Squadron in 1929 and then No.2 Training School two years later. By the end of 1932 he was in Iraq, serving in the RAF Armament Depot, before returning to Britain in 1936 for training and then a role as Armament Examining Officer, No.26 (Training) Group. On the outbreak of WW2, John Marson was a Squadron Leader and Senior Armament Officer with Headquarters Reserve Command and then transferred to the RAF's Technical Branch in April 1940. Promoted to Wing Commander, he spent most of the war as a Senior

Armament Officer at HQ Technical Training Command, and his knowledge would have been put to good use in the installation of gunnery training facilities at the incomplete Morpeth aerodrome and establishing air-to-air firing ranges along Druridge Bay for use by the unit that would be transferred or established at the station.

A small Ident & Orderly Working Party was also set up at Headquarters, Flying Training Command, involving one Equipment Officer, three assistants and three clerks. This was presumably to ensure the smooth arrival of personnel, equipment, aircraft and vehicles at RAF Morpeth. The first of these staff members turned up at the airfield on 10th March. During the remainder of that month, the Station Adjutant, Senior Accountant Officer and Station Administrative Officer all arrived. As far as flying staff were concerned, Squadron Leader G. E. Proctor was posted in on the 16th to command that aspect of operations. However, the airfield was still not at the stage where training could commence, and a number of progress meetings were therefore held by senior officers tasked with getting things up and running as soon as possible. The war was not going to wait for the new aerodrome to be completely finished, so corners had to be cut in order to allow gunnery training to start as soon as was practically possible. As the purpose-built compounds had yet to be completed, permission was given on 24th March 1942 for No.4 Site to become a temporary WAAF Site.

Other essential buildings were still in the process of being constructed too, as the Airmen's Mess did not open until the 28th - one wonders whether field kitchens had been used at the site up until then. The Sergeants already stationed at Morpeth had to wait a further week before their own Mess building could be finished by the contractors. The Senior Medical Officer, Flight Lieutenant W. J. Page, arrived on 6th April 1942. He soon learned that the station's facilities were not conducive to the health of those posted there.
Wing Commander Marson's appointment was only ever going to be a temporary one until such time as the facilities at Morpeth were brought up to a level deemed suitable for training to begin. He was therefore replaced by Wing Commander Charles Brandon on 9th April 1942, who had arrived three days earlier to allow a hand-over

period to occur. Wing Commander Marson left to take over command at No.8 Air Gunners School based at Evanton, near Dingwall in Ross & Cromarty, Scotland. Squadron Leader Proctor also departed at the same time, being replaced on the 14th by Squadron Leader A. E. Smith as Officer Commanding, Flying. In addition, Squadron Leader R. F. Helm arrived to charge of flying control duties, which would become vitally important with so many aircraft being based at Morpeth, and large numbers taking off and landing at the same time, although no Watch Office (control tower) had been built at the station at that time.

Wing Commander Charles H. Brandon, who commanded RAF Morpeth from April to June 1942. After departing the station, he was in charge of No.8 Air Gunners School at Evanton, north of Inverness, before taking command of No.210 Squadron, RAF Coastal Command, in January 1943. Charles Brandon died prematurely in November 1944, at the age of 30.

As a teenager, Morpeth resident Jack Thompson visited the newly constructed station one wet Saturday afternoon in April 1942, just before training had commenced in earnest: "A few Blackburn Bothas had arrived and one was delivered that afternoon, the ferry pilot leaving in an Air Transport Auxiliary (ATA) de Havilland Hornet Moth." Also noted visiting Morpeth that day was an air-sea-rescue Boulton-Paul Defiant from No.281 Squadron based at RAF Ouston. It was still painted in its original black night-fighter scheme, so its small red serial number was unreadable. At this time, the public road through the camp was still open, but this was soon closed once the gunnery training started in earnest. Jack plucked up the courage to accost a sergeant wearing an observer's brevet, who told him that he was on a refresher course at Morpeth. Asked what he had been flying in, the reply was informative:

"Fortresses... no bloody good! Bothas.... They're no bloody good, either!"

Presumably, the sergeant had served with No.90 Squadron, which operated the Boeing Fortress Mk.I, the British version of the B-17C Flying Fortress. 20 examples had been supplied from the United States under Lend-Lease in April 1941. The RAF had trialled the type in the high-altitude day bombing role against the wishes of the US Army Air Corps, who had advised the British to delay their introduction because of numerous faults and teething troubles in the airframes. The Americans had not yet flown the type operationally themselves at that time. No.90 Squadron lost several aircraft due to enemy action and unexplained accidents over the United Kingdom, prompting the RAF to withdraw the Fortress Mk.I in September 1941. If the unfortunate airmen that Jack Thompson had spoken to was a former B-17C navigator, his posting to Morpeth meant he was going to fly in aircraft that were equally as unloved by aircrew unlucky enough to operate them. At least there would be little or no chance of German fighters shooting them down over southern Northumberland, though. However, the risk of losses through enemy action would become the least of all worries for those assigned to the new No.4 Air Gunners School.

AN INAUSPICIOUS START: APRIL & MAY 1942

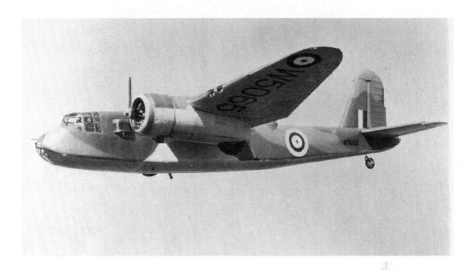

Blackburn Botha Mk.I W5065 did not serve at Morpeth but is shown here as it is representative of the examples that did. One of the aircraft's two underpowered Bristol Perseus Mk.XA radial engines can be seen: problems with these powerplants would plague maintenance crews and aircrew, leading to numerous crashes and fatalities. The Frazer-Nash mid-upper gun turret's mounting can just be made out behind the inner wing trailing edge in the photograph. It was designed to carry two machine-guns, but at Morpeth only one was usually fitted as supplies were frequently scarce due to shortages in operational bomber squadrons. (Crown Copyright expired)

No.4 Air Gunners School was established at RAF Morpeth during the middle of April 1942. The unit's first aeroplane was on its way to RAF Morpeth before the aerodrome was actually ready to accommodate its first course of pupils, although it did not reach its destination. Blackburn Botha Mk.I W5134 crashed into trees at South Clarewood, near RAF Ouston, just west of Newcastle on 11th April 1942, whilst on its delivery flight from No.33 Maintenance Unit (MU) at RAF Lyneham in Wiltshire, via No.12 MU at RAF

Kirkbride in Cumbria. The pilot, First Officer Ursula Preston, a civilian ferry pilot with the Air Transport Auxiliary, could not maintain height due to power loss from the engines. A member of the organisation's No.6 Ferry Pilots Pool, she was badly injured in the incident and the Botha was written off. Ursula Preston was an experienced pilot, having joined the ATA in June 1940. She returned to flying two months later with a glowing report from her commanding officer:

"Her accident does not seem to have affected her confidence or ability at all. Is wisely going slow on fresh types. An excellent officer."

However, the loss of their first aircraft was not a good start for the new training unit at Morpeth. At around midday on 12th April 1942, the first aircraft earmarked for RAF Morpeth actually landed at the station. These were Westland Lysander TT Mk.Is R2597 and T1563 (incorrectly listed as "J1563" in the official No.4 Air Gunners School records). They were ferried in by ATA pilots, one being First Officer Radcliffe. Two Blackburn Bothas, W5133 and W5146, also turned up later that day, whilst Lysander T4736 arrived on the 13th. The first pilot was posted in on 14th April, Pilot Officer J. Jakubowski being the first of numerous Polish airmen based at the station. A further pair of Lysanders, R9070 and T1506, landed on the 15th.

The estimated number of personnel at Morpeth had grown by this stage to around 200 of all ranks. No.4 Air Gunners School was destined to train gunners for the four-engined "heavies" of RAF Bomber Command, such as the Short Stirling, Handley Page Halifax, and Avro Lancaster, and also the various Coastal Command types such as the Armstrong-Whitworth Whitley, Boeing Fortress and Short Sunderland.

The School was to be equipped with the Blackburn Botha. This was a twin-engined light torpedo bomber and reconnaissance aircraft that had recently been withdrawn from front-line service. The Botha was a high-winged monoplane fitted with two 930hp Bristol Perseus Mk.XA engines, the nacelles of which created blind spots for the pilot to the side and rear of the aircraft. A gun turret located on the top of the rear fuselage was fitted with two Vickers machine-guns, and the pilot had a forward firing 0.303-inch machine-gun. Provision for a single torpedo or up to 2000lbs of bombs was made in an internal fuselage bay. Even with the 930hp engines, which had replaced the type's original 830hp powerplants, the aircraft was desperately underpowered and was not a success in operational service.

Another image of a Botha, this time a close-up of the cockpit area showing the bomb aimer's position in the glazed nose. A single machine-gun was installed in operational aircraft, but this was surplus to requirements for gunnery training and usually removed. The airman, date and location are all unknown, although the photograph could have easily been taken on one of the remote parking "pans" at Morpeth. (Unknown)

Only one squadron actually flew the type, No.608 ("North Riding") Squadron, based at RAF Thornaby. Thirty different Bothas were flown from there between June and November 1940 before the aircraft were sent to various MUs for storage and reallocation to training units. Whilst its handling and engine power were judged to be unsatisfactory for front-line operations, the type was considered to be reasonably useful in the gunnery-training role as a mid-upper gun turret was fitted, and each aircraft could carry a number of pupils during each flight. The runways at Morpeth were just long enough for a Botha to use, and take-offs invariably used practically all of the available distance. Pilots therefore elected to taxi right to the threshold in order to make sure there was enough for them to take-off safely. Training units simply had to make do with cast-offs, obsolete types or knackered aircraft that had been flogged to death in front-line service. It did not bode well for the new unit.

Plans called for twenty-seven Bothas to be delivered to No.4 Air Gunners School as the unit's initial establishment, together with an immediate reserve of thirteen aircraft. The latter was probably deemed necessary given the attrition rate that No.608 Squadron had experienced when operating the type. Events would soon prove this decision to be correct. Fourteen Westland Lysander target tugs were also to be delivered. Seven further Lysanders would also be retained as a reserve.

The fledgling air gunners were to attend a six week-long course at RAF Morpeth, which would involve classroom lectures and, providing they were graded as suitable to continue the course, gunnery training at the air-to-air firing ranges located over the sea off Druridge Bay, between Amble and Lynemouth. The School's aircraft flew a regular route to and from these ranges and very rarely strayed too far from this area. This often involved flying from Morpeth to Blyth, and then up the coast to the range at Druridge Bay, crossing the coast near Alnmouth and returning to the station via an inland route.

On 16th April, the day before No.4 Air Gunners School was supposed to officially open, Botha W5148 arrived at Morpeth, swelling the numbers of the School's aircraft to eight. However, pupils for the first gunnery course were not due to arrive for a couple of weeks, which gave the hard-pressed station staff more precious time with which to prepare the airfield and its facilities for duty. Two further pairs of aircraft turned up on the 22nd, Lysanders R2575 and R2578, followed by Bothas W5145 and W5147. Due to the dimensions of the turret fitted to the Botha aircraft, a height limit was imposed on trainees posted to No.4 Air Gunners School. Each one completed an average of fifteen flights. On completion of their course, the newly-qualified gunners would then be posted to an Operational Training Unit to form part of a newly formed bomber crew which would eventually move onto a front-line squadron, either in Britain or in the Mediterranean.

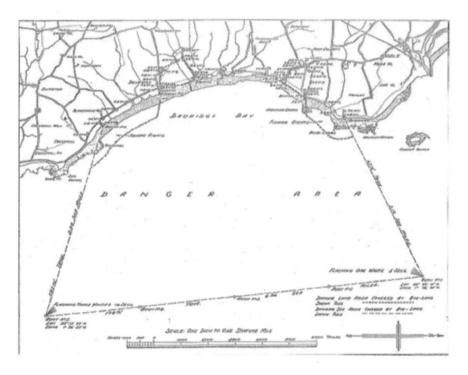

An official map of the gunnery ranges off Druridge Bay, Northumberland.

Aerial target towing was to be performed out over the North Sea, at various points from the Farne Islands down to the River Tyne, with three areas including the one off Druridge Bay being used for this purpose. Another was situated off Amble. Drogue targets would be used instead of flags, many being lost due to problems with winch-brake failure or bullets hitting the towlines. Drogues were usually towed at a distance of 1,000 feet or more behind the tug to maintain a decent margin of safety, as it was not unknown for trainees to accidentally open fire when pointing the turret in the wrong direction. The Westland Lysander and later Miles Martinet target tug pilots were to drop their drogues at a site at Amble before returning to Morpeth. A detachment from No.4 Air Gunners School based at Amble would then collect each target and counted the paint-circled holes in each one before telephoning the airfield with the relevant scores.

Some initial training flights involved Bothas landing at Boulmer, which had opened as a satellite landing ground for the Spitfires of No.57 Operational Training Unit at Eshott in March 1942. Being refuelled and rearmed at another station, this effectively doubled the amount of training the pupils could receive from a single training flight and speeded up the courses at Morpeth. However, once No.57 Operational Training Unit began to outgrow Eshott, they transferred their Advanced Flight across to Boulmer and so there was less airspace in the landing circuit for the Bothas and fewer spare personnel to attend to them. Eventually, No.4 Air Gunners School had to all but cease using the coastal site during training flights. The aerodrome at Boulmer was south of the post-war helicopter search-and-rescue base, and the former line of the old main north-south runway can still be seen today.

A ground firing range for the trainee gunners was established on the coast at North Seaton, between Cambois and Newbiggin-by-the-Sea. It was adjacent to the sea and featured a narrow-gauge railway along which targets were moved back and forth. Pupils were driven across from Morpeth to North Seaton on most days for training. The range was laid out so that they fired out to sea, no doubt in order to avoid any embarrassing episodes! An illuminated night target was also set up at Sandy Bay, located on a two-hundred-yard-long moving range. However, night flying did not commence from Morpeth for some time. The range at North Seaton is now the location of a large caravan site.

No.4 Air Gunners School was officially allowed to devise its own system for identifying its aircraft, with the sole proviso that they did not adopt three-letter codes. This was in order to prevent confusion with the codes used by operational squadrons, and the School eventually settled on a simple numerical system. Pupils at Morpeth usually completed around fifteen flights before gaining their brevets. They also attended swimming baths in Ashington and Newcastle to receive wet dinghy training. It was important that the gunners learn how to extricate themselves from their ditched aircraft and into an inflatable dinghy if their aircraft had to be put down in the sea.

On 1st May 1942, the numbers of station personnel were recorded as follows: 32 officers, 52 senior non-commissioned officers, 347 airmen and 32 airwomen. Four days later, Air Chief Marshal Sir Edgar Ludlow-Hewitt arrived at RAF Morpeth to inspect the newly commissioned airfield. He flew in from nearby Acklington at 1055 hours, departing just 90 minutes later by road for the RAF School of Administration at Stannington, a couple of miles away to the east. There may have been little for him to inspect since the station was yet to accept its first gunnery trainees. Electricity, gas and water supplies had been promised but had still not been connected some of the station's buildings by this time, including the Station Sick Quarters. It is not known whether the Air Chief Marshal was informed about this or some of the other pressing problems affecting the station.

Ablutions (toilet, showering and washing facilities) were initially only available at the Communal Site, which meant that personnel billeted or assigned to duties elsewhere across the station were faced with a long walk every time they were required. The medical staff noticed that some airmen were failing to wash due to the prospect of early-morning long distance walks in poor weather conditions to do so. Worse still, water samples taken in mid-March 1942 had proved to be contaminated by sewerage, forcing all supplies drawn at the station to be boiled before use. Although further samples taken in April showed no contamination, boiling of water continued into May as further construction and extension work on the pipework was taking place. The station's sewerage plant, a modern sludge-type facility, was virtually complete by 1st May 1942, allowing connections to be made to the Communal Site, Station Sick Quarters, No.4 Site and No.1 WAAF site, the latter which was still not ready for use. All of the other sites continued to use Elsan toilets until they were finally connected much later.

A close up of the water tower building on WAAF Site No.1. The two toilets can be easily made out in this photograph. The original pipework running out of the structure has long since disappeared, leaving only short stubs still projecting from the side wall. The photo was taken in August 2021. (Author)

At the beginning of May 1942, lighting on the station was still provided by paraffin lamps only, as the electricity supply had not been connected. However, food was at least plentiful, and the meals provided at the Airmen's Mess were described as "excellent", "a compensation for many hardships." All ranks were eating their meals there, as the Officers Mess would not be completed until the first week of June 1942. An electricity supply was finally established on 18th May, much to the delight of the station personnel.

7th May 1942 saw the first of many flying accidents at RAF Morpeth. Flight Sergeant Lee in Botha W5133 touched down on one of the runways but ran off onto the soft grass, causing his port wheel to sink. The port undercarriage leg was not bent in the actual incident, but a stringer was damaged when the aircraft was recovered, perhaps by inexperienced personnel. They would soon get plenty of practice, starting with Lysander R2576, which crashed on landing just three days later. The starboard undercarriage was damaged but later repaired, and the pilot walked away unscathed.

An inspection of the buildings at the Amble Range left the station's Senior Medical Officer distinctly unimpressed:

"This range has been handed over in a very dirty condition, especially kitchen and cooking utensils. Refuse dump in a brick hut was filled with old tins and consequently rat-infested. Blankets very dirty. Action being taken to remedy these matters."

Squadron Officer Lady Chetwynd was another important visitor, this time on 15th May 1942 when she inspected the WAAFs' quarters. If any of the airwomen had fallen ill at that time, they would have been forced to use one of three bunks earmarked for use on No.4 Site, the temporary WAAF site. A dedicated building was still not ready for them. Rounding off the VIP visits during the month, Viscount Trenchard arrived on the following day to inspect the new aerodrome. Their actual comments have not been recorded.

The unit lost its first Lysander target tug on the 17th when L4736 crashed at Saltwick, not far from the southern edge of the aerodrome. The aircraft stalled when its Bristol Mercury XII engine failed, causing it to hit the ground. The accident card for this event reads as follows:

"A/C climbed 800-1,000 ft where engine cut, pilot appeared to be attempting a normal forced landing into wind but stalled a/c from 50 ft and was unable to recover."

The pilot, Flight Sergeant H. Szwedowski, was criticised for not checking the amount of engine coolant being carried in the Lysander, the lack of which may have contributed to its sudden failure. However, it was judged not to be a material factor in the crash. The Polish pilot was quickly transferred to Newcastle General Hospital for treatment. He had received serious injuries, including skull and tibia factures, and subsequently never flew again.

The difficulties encountered in preparing RAF Morpeth for use by pupils meant that the initial group of 45 airmen comprising No.1 Course did not arrive at the station until 23rd May 1942. Most, if not all, would have arrived by train at Morpeth station, the fortunate ones taking advantage of arranged transport or cadging a lift. For those who were unlucky enough to turn up late for the free rides, there was always the option of the three or so mile walk to the aerodrome main gate. 24th May 1942 was presumably an orientation day for the new trainees, as No.1 Course did not commence until the following day.

Once at the station and processed, the personnel for each course were separated out into squads of six airmen. These groups would stick together throughout the remainder of the syllabus. Each Botha could carry three trainee gunners so two were needed for each squad per practice session. The airmen were issued with flying kit, although their caps had a white flash to denote their trainee status. They were usually promoted to Leading Aircraftsman at this stage and given a badge with a single propeller marked on it. This had to be sewn onto their uniform: needlework was therefore another skill learned by many young men at Morpeth. The trainee gunners also had to perform non-flying duties such as guarding aircraft, installations and buildings, peeling potatoes for the mess hall, cleaning coal buckets and any other "make work" tasks that their superiors saw fit to assign to them. In addition, there were also the usual physical training sessions and marching drills to fit in around training flights. There was always plenty to do when the trainees were not airborne, attending ground lectures or conducting firing drills. Following a night of two-hours-on and four-hours-off guard duty, some pupils found it somewhat difficult to concentrate on their ground lectures and flying exercises.

Royal Canadian Air Force Westland Lysander TT Mk.II 1557, pictured in British Columbia during February 1944. It is representative of the aircraft based at Morpeth in 1942 and 1943. The aircraft wore black and yellow diagonal stripe markings so that they stood out, in order that trainees would notice them when firing at the drogue targets. (Creative Commons)

Before the trainees were let loose on the guns, many hours of study were needed on the ground. First came classroom lectures on aircraft recognition, map reading, basic navigation and maths. Classes also involved RAF law and administration. Training films, such as the 1940 Air Gunners training film that was shot showing personnel manning turrets on Boulton-Paul Defiant fighters and Vickers Wellington bombers, were also part of the curriculum. The trainees then had to become familiar in handling the guns themselves, which involved instruction in several different types, from the 0.303-inch Vickers K to the similar calibre M1919 Browning Mk.II. Ground training in the Frazer-Nash turrets installed in the Standard Free Gunnery trainer buildings followed. Further classroom lectures added to the experience gained in the ground-based turrets, explaining the terms "curve of pursuit", "estimation of deflection" and "bullet drop" to the trainees. These were all technical terms involved in sighting, aiming and firing at enemy aircraft.

Conservation of ammunition was emphasised by the instructors. A one-second burst of fire usually expended ten rounds and keeping one's finger on the trigger simply "hosepiped" bullets instead of laying them accurately on target. A 0.303-inch Browning was capable of firing 1,200 rounds a minute, but there was only room in the turret for ammunition boxes carrying around 10,000 rounds in total. Short, sharp bursts were therefore more effective and prevented gunners from quickly running out of ammo. Trainees also had to learn how to strip down a Browning Mk.II machine-gun to its component parts and put them all back together again. They were then timed, and after becoming proficient, were timed again, this time wearing blindfolds. After all, they would be expected to fix any jams that occurred on missions whilst flying in the dark.

Once these skills had been mastered, it was time for the pupils to start practising their skills in a live aircraft. The "hit" ratio for firing at towed drogue targets was surprisingly low, around 7% being considered good enough for a pass to be given. The level was calculated on the number of bullet strikes that were needed to bring an enemy aircraft down. Trainees carried around 200 rounds of ammunition with them on practice flights in the Bothas, so providing more than 14 "hits" were counted, they were not washed out of the course. However, the special colours painted onto the tips of the bullets to signify who had fired them did not always register on the holes in the drogues, much to the annoyance of the trainees. A typical month's flights experienced by a gunnery trainee at Morpeth can be summed up as follows:

Air to Sea, Buoys (no rounds fired) 40 minutes
Air to Air, Beam (no rounds fired, 1 hour 5 mins)
Air to Air, Beam (200 rounds, 1 hour 30 mins)
Air to Air, Beam (100 rounds,1 hour 20 mins)
Air to Air, Undertail (100 rounds, 1 hour 20 mins)
Air to Air, Undertail (200 rounds, 1 hour)
Air to Air, Undertail (200 rounds, 35 mins)
Air to Air, Observation of Tracer (200 rounds, 55 mins)
Air to Air, Observation of Tracer (200 rounds, 1 hour)
Air to Air (Tracer), Undertail (200 rounds, 55 mins)
Air to Air (Tracer), Undertail (200 rounds, 1 hour 15 mins)
Air to Air (Tracer), Beam Apparent Relative Speed
(no target, 50 minutes)

The Bothas carried the standard RAF Training Command colours of "trainer yellow" undersides and camouflaged upper surfaces, these being dark earth and dark green. Individual aircraft numbers were painted in blue behind the fuselage roundels. The aircraft were also fitted with the early wartime gas detector panels, which came in the form of a small yellow diamond outlined in black on top of the fuselage just forward of the tail fin. No.4 Air Gunners School also operated a single Fairey Battle Trainer, serial number P6666, which arrived at Morpeth in August 1942 and served with the unit until November of the same year. This was used by the tug pilots for training duties, so that the Lysanders did not have to be diverted to other tasks.

The trainee gunners comprising No.1 Course may have got to hear about the inauspicious start to Botha operations with the loss of the Air Gunners School's first aircraft before it even arrived at the station via some of the "old sweats". Those watching the flying activities taking place on 24th May 1942 would have been even further dismayed to see W5146 being blown over on take-off. The following note appeared in the No.4 Air Gunners School records:

"The wind had got under the tail. Fuselage damaged from nose to frame 'E'. Engines shock-loaded, propellers bent."

The pilot, Sergeant Glowacki, and his passenger, Sergeant Garstecki, both Polish, were happily uninjured in the incident, and the personnel assigned to the recovery detail received much-needed practice in retrieving bent airframes.

With accidents such as this one occurring before the training programme had even begun, plans to create a reserve of Botha aircraft sounded more and more sound by the day. However, worse was yet to come, as a second Lysander was damaged beyond repair on the 30th when R2575 crashed on landing. The aircraft bounced whilst touching down in a crosswind and overturned. Flight Lieutenant R. Lutoslawski was admitted to the Station Sick Quarters suffering from shock, plus conjunctivitis caused by fuel from the aircraft's ruptured tanks getting into his eyes.

Morpeth received further VIP visitors on 25th May 1942 when the Under Secretary of State for Air, Lord Sherwood, plus his Parliamentary Private Secretary, Viscount Cowdray, arrived at the station by air for an inspection. It is not known what their findings were.

Although the various flying departments had improved in advance of No.1 Course starting, the same could not be said about many of the station's buildings in April and May 1942. The medical unit comprised the Senior Medical Officer, Flight Lieutenant Page, plus four non-commissioned officers and five airmen. The Station Sick Quarters building was still not completed, as an annexe was yet to be finished, but at least they were able to use most of the structure. It boasted a 12-bed main ward, a two-bed officers' ward and a small isolation ward. Two separate dental surgeries had been created but they could not function as no Dental Officer had been assigned to RAF Morpeth. However, there was some good news, as three ambulances had arrived at Morpeth for use by No.4 Air Gunners School. One, an Albion, was kept at permanent readiness as a crash tender on the airfield in case of incidents, a Morris was assigned to Station Sick Quarters and a third (still undergoing repairs) was destined for Amble, where the small contingent assigned to the coastal ranges was billeted.

UP & RUNNING:
JUNE & JULY 1942

Another photograph showing the pilot's "office" in a Blackburn Botha torpedo bomber. This is another undated image and again the location is unknown. It could well have been taken at Morpeth although the flat land in the background suggests somewhere else entirely. (Unknown)

The flying training programme at Morpeth finally got going on 31st May 1942 with the first of the No.1 Course pupil gunners taking their initial trips in the School's Botha aircraft. Collectively, they fired some 2,100 rounds that day. The station itself had grown to a complement of 764, plus the 45 trainees. There were 39 officers, 84 senior non-commissioned officers, a solitary WAAF senior non-commissioned officer, 545 airmen and 95 airwomen, excluding the trainees. It was always intended to have several gunners' courses running at the same time, albeit at different stages. The 45 pupils posted to No.2 Course on 7th June and an identical number turned up on the 13th for No.3. No.1 Course ended on the 4th, with all 45 trainees passing to become qualified air gunners. Each one had fired on average 1,800 rounds in air-to-air firing and another 150 in air-to-ground practice. Their success came despite no cine-camera or Spotlight trainer aids being available at the time. Such equipment (known in the RAF as "synthetic aids") would not appear until later.

Two airmen were recommended to be retained as instructors, which was a recognised practice in training units. The cream of the crop was often kept from operational duties - at least for a short while - because it was more efficient to have them pass on their own recent expertise and they could also emphasise with the difficulties experienced by the following batches of trainees.

Another Polish pilot, Josef Jaworzyn, was posted to the staff of No.4 Air Gunners School in 1942. After the war, he wrote the book *No Place To Land* about his experiences as a Coastal Command pilot, flying long sorties over the North Atlantic in search of U-boats. It also included information about his time at Morpeth, which he described thus:

"A disappointment (...) Our living quarters were nearly a mile from the messes, which in turn were a mile from the aerodrome."

He did not have anything good to say about the airfield's layout, either:

"The runways were cut through woods and built on a bog. There was one hangar, plus a curiously off-centre Flying Control, which considering all the obstructions, was not very effective."

However, Jaworzyn saved his ire for the Botha aircraft that he had to fly in. He summed up the type as follows:

"A scrap metal dealer or ship designer had been involved in their construction. The torpedo bay was off centre, the wings small and

the engines so underpowered that any pilot who flew one will no doubt remember it to this day."

The Pole was equally unimpressed with the close proximity of Newcastle's anti-aircraft defences, trying to stay clear of them at all costs:

"It was an important harbour, something we did not have to be told too often. The air above the town was packed with barrage balloons, and we had observed the anti-aircraft guns in action on occasion, not necessarily against hostile aircraft."

September 2021: a view south-westwards along what used to be Runway 23 at RAF Morpeth. The tarmac surface is extremely broken up here. This section is however used for car boot sales on Sunday afternoons between late March and the end of September each year. Parking for visitors takes place on the old north-western perimeter track, behind and to the right. (Author)

17th June 1942 saw two incidents involving No.4 Air Gunners School aircraft, thankfully with no resulting casualties. Lysander R2576, flown by Sergeant D. G. Turner, was taxying on the runway when it was caught by a gust of wind which blew the aircraft off the tarmac and onto the grass. The wheels dug into the soft ground and the aircraft tipped onto its nose, damaging the propeller blades. Another incident occurred on the same day, this time involving Botha W5153, which landed in a field near Benridge Mill to the north of Mitford, due to a failure in the aircraft's fuel supply system. According to details learned at the time, the pilot had taken off with the fuel cocks switched off, which was against procedure. None of the crew was hurt but Pilot Officer Ryszard Reszko faced a Court of Inquiry due to possible negligence. Eventually re-instated, he was however killed in a crash at Morpeth on 22nd June 1943. Josef Jaworzyn had witnessed some of the second incident as he stood on the aerodrome:

"We saw the aircraft wobble, heard the engines splutter, and in seconds the plane had disappeared behind the hills. The ambulance and the crash party tore away noisily, returning with Reszko. He was unruffled, and back in time for his second trip of the day."

Reszko, his gunnery instructor, Sergeant Moon, plus the three trainee gunners onboard W5153 all escaped unscathed from the forced landing.

Wing Commander Brandon had been promoted from the rank of Squadron Leader in September 1941 at the age of 27. Again, his tenure at Morpeth was short, as he was replaced on 20th June 1942, moving to No.1 Air Armament School at RAF Manby in Lincolnshire. He would die of natural causes in July 1944, aged just 30. His successor was Wing Commander Richard I. Jones, who had joined the RAF as a flight cadet in 1933. In 1935 he was posted to No.29 Squadron at North Weald in Essex, where he flew two-seater Hawker Demon biplane fighters, before becoming a flight instructor with No.3 Flying Training School in November 1936. As a Flight Lieutenant, Jones joined No.4 Bombing & Gunnery School at RAF

West Freugh, near Stranraer, before being promoted to Squadron Leader and transferring to No.9 Bombing & Gunnery School at Penhros in North Wales as their new Armament Officer in October 1940. In February 1942 he took up the post of Officer Commanding, B Flight, No.1 Air Armament School at Manby in Lincolnshire. This unit carried out specialist training with bombing ranges off the coast at Wainfleet and Donna Nook. After a long post-war RAF career, Richard Jones ended up as an Air Vice-Marshal, taking over command of No.11 Group in April 1968, before retiring two years later. No sooner had Wing Commander Jones settled into his new command than his own boss, Officer Commanding No.29 (Flying Training) Group, Air Commodore Norton, turned up for an inspection. He lunched in the new Officers Mess and left by air after a successful visit.

One of the Lysanders spent less than two months with the School before being written off. At around 1630 hours on 26th June, L4733 was returning to Morpeth on completion of a drogue towing flight. Its pilot, Sergeant K. M. Davey, apparently approached the runway too high and also too fast. He overshot the landing and then swung to avoid the boundary fence but struck a hedge in the process. The force of the impact damaged the Lysander's undercarriage and then overturned the aircraft completely. The target tug finally came to rest upside-down on the Saltwick to Mitford road, completely blocking it. The aircraft was removed, and the road was re-opened some three hours later. Davey's commanding officer stated that the pilot had "failed to take overshoot action", in that he had not aborted the landing and gone around again for another attempt. The commanding officer at Morpeth simply added one word to the report: *"Carelessness"*. It was lucky that no-one on the road itself was injured or killed, considering that it was still open to the public at the time. A good view of activities at RAF Morpeth could be seen by passing cyclists and drivers for several months after the aerodrome opened, but the Saltwick to Mitford road was eventually closed to civilian traffic, with local farmers being exempt. On the same day, Botha L6247 came to grief whilst landing, but pilot Sergeant Jedliczko was uninjured.

No.4 Course turned up the following day with another 45 trainees, as was by now the standard number. No.4 Air Gunners School came under the control of No.29 (Flying Training) Group at Dumfries which looked after all of the Air Gunner Schools and Advanced Flying Units in northern England. Many of the pilots assigned to fly the unit's Bothas at Morpeth were Polish; most of them found this duty tedious, compared with flying front-line missions against the Germans. This monotony, accompanied with some bouts of low-level flying over the local countryside and "beat-ups" (low passes) over the nearby town of Morpeth, together with a lack of proper flying control and the poor performance of the Botha, quickly led to a succession of incidents at the station.

Ian Tapster, who wrote a couple of articles for the *Morpeth Herald* in 2002 about the aerodrome, mentioned that his brother-in-law, who as a boy of twelve in 1942, lived near Alnwick:

"He was raking hay in a hollow on his father's farm on Alnwick Moor when a Botha roared in from the coast below treetop height."

Inevitably, accidents involving aircraft belonging to No.4 Air Gunners School were numerous and are listed at the end of this book. At the end of June 1942, it was decided that local Air Training Corps squadrons would be attached to RAF Morpeth for summer camps from mid-July until the end of August. It was recognised that many of the cadets would end up as aircrew, and were potential air gunners, so allowing them basic exposure to training procedures would be beneficial to all concerned. Trainees from the actual courses underway during June 1942 were adapting well and getting to grips with becoming fully-fledged air gunners. They expended some 110,000 rounds of ammunition during training flights and another 74,700 in ground firing, using a makeshift range located a couple of miles from the station as the large firing butts had not yet been completed.

A further inspection of the Amble facilities found that the previous discrepancies had been remedied and that the site was fit for occupation. Although they had an ambulance assigned to RAF Morpeth, any casualties were to be taken to Alnwick Infirmary for treatment.

An aerial view of RAF Morpeth, looking south-west, taken from one of No.4 Air Gunners School's Lysander aircraft on 29th July 1942. At least 36 Blackburn Bothas can be made out on the image although there are none parked outside the Blister hangars on the southern "loop". (Unknown)

July brought no respite to the crash recovery teams at Morpeth. The month started badly when Sergeant Garstecki clipped a tree whilst landing in Botha W5121. The aircraft's bomb bay doors were damaged and required repair or replacement. This was Garstecki's second incident as he had been a passenger during one in May 1942. Two days later, Sergeant Switalski, another Polish pilot, swung and struck a paint sprayer after suffering brake failure whilst taxying after landing. Damage was sustained to the starboard tailplane and the propeller blades, the latter being fractured.

This incident presumably did not affect the No.1 Course passing out parade too much, and Bomber Command received 43 new air gunners which were sorely needed for the ever-expanding number of operational squadrons. No sooner had these airmen left the station than No.5 Course arrived, again seeing another 45 cadets looking forward to several weeks of training. A medical officer arrived on the 10th to carry out what was known as "swing testing", where a group of trainees was presumably swung about in order to see whether they would become airsick. There had already been fifteen cases reported to the station's Senior Medical Officer and the amount of flying in the courses had been determined as insufficient to show whether or not airmen would "get over it".

On the 11th, a camouflage and decoy officer arrived to see what could be done about making the buildings less conspicuous from the air. The following day, the No.29 Group Defence Officer turned up to inspect the airfield's ability to repel any attacking or invading German forces. Shortly afterwards, No.29 Group brought RAF Morpeth into the *Banquet* organisation, which meant that if required due to impending invasion or other such emergencies, the Bothas of No.4 Air Gunners School could be placed under the control of No.18 Group, Coastal Command. This emergency plan called for training aircraft to be placed on an operational footing, using instructors and also pupils in the advanced stages of their courses to form squadrons to augment the front-line units. Plans for No.4 Air Gunners School involved fourteen Bothas, crewed by No.29 Group personnel and ready to carry out simple bombing operations within fifty miles of the coast. It will be remembered that the Botha had already seen service in Coastal Command, albeit with just one squadron, No.608, so the aircraft was built, although not necessarily suited, for the task. If the war situation had dictated that the *Banquet* plans were to be implemented, then the underground battle headquarters building would have been used. Built to Air Ministry Drawing Number 11008/41, this structure was located just outside the extreme southwest comer of the aerodrome, just north of an old quarry. From this building, the defence of RAF Morpeth would have been directed, the only part visible being the above ground observation post with its firing slits.

No.2 Course passed out on 18th July, with just one of the 45 airmen failing to pass the course. He was posted to Blackpool for reassignment to other duties. No.6 turned up to replace them, this time with 60 airmen. 66 cadets from No.167 (Seaton Delaval) Squadron, Air Training Corps, also arrived for their week's Summer Camp. Morpeth was becoming a much busier place. Gunnery training started to be a more routine business, with No.3 Course passing out on 25th and No.7 arriving later the same day. At any one time, there were four separate courses at the station. No.1000 Squadron (Ashington) Air Training Corps also turned up for their own Summer Camp.

On 28th July, the Morpeth crash and rescue team had the dubious privilege of dealing with an aircraft not based at their station. A Hawker Hurricane Mk.I from No.59 Operational Training Unit based at RAF Crosby-on-Eden (now Carlisle Airport) force-landed on the airfield after a defective engine connecting rod was pushed through the sump. The aircraft's undercarriage collapsed on landing. It is not known which particular Hurricane was involved as the serial is given as "MF.7178", which was not one assigned to the type.

Sergeant Garstecki was beginning to acquire a reputation as an unlucky pilot. He ended the month as he had started it, being involved in a third flying incident. On this occasion, Botha W5139 was damaged in mid-air whilst flying over one of the gunnery ranges off the Northumberland coast. Spent ammunition casings ejected from the aircraft struck the starboard propeller, damaging it.

EXERCISE *DRYSHOD*: AUGUST 1942

A line-up of No.72 Squadron Spitfire Mk.VBs pictured in 1941. (Unknown)

No.72 Squadron's Spitfire Mk.IXs were briefly based at Morpeth between 4th and 12th August 1942 for Exercise *Dryshod*, prior to the unit re-equipping with Mk.Vs whilst at Ayr and later Ouston, in preparation for a move to Algeria and Tunisia. The ground element travelled by rail at 1900 hours on 1st August 1942 from the squadron's base at Biggin Hill after the day's last operation, a fighter sweep and escort of bombers over the Channel. Around 200 personnel from the squadron would eventually be accommodated at RAF Morpeth for the exercise.

The Spitfires should have reached Morpeth on the 2nd, but bad weather delayed their departure from Biggin until 1605 hours that day, so the pilots only aimed for Church Fenton in North Yorkshire before having to stop for the night. However, even this limited objective was impossible as poor weather forced them to turn back after an hour and land at Duxford in Cambridgeshire, as it was the only station near enough that could service Spitfires. The squadron's Miles Magister, with two of the unit's Sergeant pilots aboard, got as far as Grimsby before having to land.

Happily, No.72 Squadron's ground party did reach RAF Morpeth at around 1900 on the 2nd and began to settle in. Two Handley-Page Harrows from No.271 Squadron, K7009 and K7032, arrived at Morpeth at 1630 hours on 3rd August 1942, carrying the Spitfire ground crews. The aircraft had departed Biggin Hill that morning and stopped at Church Fenton en route. No.72 Squadron's Adjutant, Flying Officer Le Petit, and Medical Officer, Flying Officer Griffin, put in a lot of hard work to ensure that the unit's personnel were as comfortable as possible in their new (temporary) home, as *"many facilities did not exist or only existed in embryo, and dispersal had been carried out to a very wide extent."*

Meanwhile, at Duxford, on the 4th, Squadron Leader Bobby Oxspring, DFC, was about to receive a huge blow to his hopes of actually reaching Morpeth to participate in Exercise *Dryshod*. No.72 Squadron's record book did not hold back:

"(...) an order from Fighter Command reached them, requisitioning the twelve hydromatic propellers previously fitted to the squadron's aircraft. This was the final blow to our hopes as we saw these more recent and efficient propellers ripped off our aircraft, which were left useless on the aerodrome; and our prospects of taking part in Exercise Dryshod receded."

There was a last-minute reprieve, however. Twelve Spitfires from No.71 Squadron at Debden were suddenly produced and handed over to Oxspring's unit, and his squadron was therefore able to leave Duxford, finally arriving at Morpeth two days behind schedule. RAF Morpeth was now going to participate in *Dryshod* as originally planned.

The squadron's intelligence officer flew to RAF Dumfries, where the "German Army defending France" was based for the duration. He returned with useful information that explained what No.72 Squadron's role would be whilst operating out of Morpeth. The "British forces" were considered to have invaded an imaginary coastline stretching south-west to north-east from Girvan to

Edinburgh. "Bridgeheads" had been forced in the Dalmellington and Dumfries areas.

Bobby Oxspring, as drawn by Cuthbert Orde on 3rd November 1940 for the book "Pilots of Fighter Command". (Public Domain)

On the morning of 5th August 1942, one flight of No.72 Squadron's Spitfires was at readiness and another at 30 minutes readiness. At 1016 hours, a signal was received for the unit to send four aircraft to attack an armoured column on the road between Dalmellington and Carsphairn, which was moorland country. They took off at 1030 hours but returned at 1125, having been unable to reach their objective due to low cloud. A further signal in the afternoon directed six Spitfires to attack a second column near New Cumnock. Due to a misunderstanding, only four took off from Morpeth but spotted the large number of tanks and other vehicles at the target site. These were "shot up" successfully (dummy attacks, obviously!), as were two de Havilland Puss Moth aircraft which seemed to be operating in support of the column. A third signal at 1540 resulted in a further six Spitfires leaving Morpeth to attack the same target. This time they were engaged by pretend flak and the exercise umpires decreed that two of the Spitfires had been shot down, with two others damaged. All twelve of the unit's aircraft (therefore including the two "losses"!) went out again at 1830 to engage troops in Ayrshire. The first day's exercise at Morpeth had seen No.72 Squadron stand ten and a half hours at readiness and fly four sorties.

It was reported to be "very cold" at 0700 hours on the 6th. Six Spitfires left Morpeth at 0814 hours to find an armoured column north of Dumfries. A second sortie departed at 0946, looking for the same target, and worked in concert with Douglas Boston bombers. No.72 Squadron sent out a third flight at 1120, which attacked a convoy near Carsphairn. One of the Spitfire pilots nearly did not return to Morpeth, as Pilot Officer J. Lowe hit high-tension cables just south-east of Dalmellington and had to force-land his aircraft. Spitfire BM189 was adjudged beyond repair, but the pilot survived unhurt, and eventually returned to Morpeth. Despite the squadron records suggesting it was a write-off, the aircraft was salvaged and then repaired since it was delivered to the Soviet Union during December 1942. The third sortie of the day saw aircraft making dummy attacks on a column near Sanquhar, and a final group of eight Spitfires left Morpeth at 1733 hours for the Patna area. Given the success of the day's operations, the squadron was stood down until 0700 hours the following morning. However, 7th August 1942 started with heavy rain and the conditions did not improve until 1130 hours. The weather was still considered to be unfit for flying and so an order was received cancelling all operations for the rest of the day. Almost the entire squadron therefore visited Ashington where a dance was being held, and the record book states that *"a good time was had by all"*. If anyone had a sore head the following morning, at least they did not have to fly. All operations on the 8th were also scrubbed due to poor weather conditions, heavy rain making it dangerous to carry out sorties. *Dryshod* seemed to be anything but! Squadron Leader Oxspring mentioned Morpeth in his autobiography, *Spitfire Command*, stating that:

"(...) this hutted habitat was depressing."

The squadron did however receive a warm welcome from the local civilian population, who remembered their spirited defence of the region back in August 1940. Bobby Oxspring remarked that:

"(...) all ranks in the squadron soon discovered that (...) Newcastle Brown Ale had lost none of its pre-war potency!"

The 9th dawned much brighter, with 8/10th cloud at 5,000 feet. However, No.72 Squadron's part in the exercise soon ended as across in the west, the "British forces'" objectives had just been met so a "cease fire" signal was received, releasing the squadron for training flights. Any feelings that boredom might set in were quickly dispelled in the early hours of the 10th, when a line of flares were reported as being dropped from Newcastle to Blyth, and a Beaufighter had chased a *Luftwaffe* raider up the coast. After the alarm was raised, the No.72 Squadron Spitfire pilots at Morpeth were put on readiness but they were never ordered to take off. All training had been suspended in any case due to more heavy rain, and instead, No.72 Squadron's personnel concentrated on getting ready for their move to RAF Ayr in Scotland on the 12th. The advance party of ground staff departed by rail from Morpeth station on the 11th, whilst several officers left by road. The Spitfires did leave on schedule on the 12th but were almost immediately recalled by Group Headquarters and quickly landed at Ouston, just west of Newcastle. *Dryshod* had not been a great success in terms of hours flown, and the squadron had lost an aircraft, but it was considered to be a useful learning exercise. Another unit arrived at Morpeth at around the same time, but it would have an even briefer tenure at the station. No.3045 (Royal Canadian Air Force) Servicing Echelon arrived on 10th August 1942 and departed two days later.

Former Morpeth resident Jack Thompson, who was at school there, managed to obtain a close look at one of the Spitfires with some of his friends, only for the pilot, who just happened to be the unit's commanding officer, Bobby Oxspring, to give them a right rollicking! One of the Spitfire Mk.VBs, BM345, returned to Northumberland after service with No.72 Squadron in North Africa, as it was lost in an incident at Boulmer in February 1945 while serving with No.57 Operational Training Unit. Once Dryshod was over, the ground crews departed in Handley Page "Sparrows" K6987 and K7010, again machines from No.271 Squadron.

No.72 Squadron Spitfire Mk.VBs at RAF Morpeth, August 1942:

BL810 BM108 BM117 BM189 BM192 BM193 BM211
BM327 BM345 BM413 BM470 BM636

No.72 Squadron pilots at RAF Morpeth, August 1942:

Sqdn Ldr R. W. Oxspring, DFC (Commanding Officer, No.72 Sqdn)
F/Lt P. F. Colloredo-Mansfeld (American) ("A" Flight Commander)
P/O E. Budrewicz (Polish)
P/O D. G. Cox
P/O O. L. Hardy (New Zealand)
P/O J. Le Cheminant
P/O J. Lowe

P/O R. J. Robertson
F/Sgt J. W. Patterson
Sgt G. Fosse (Norwegian)
Sgt P. R. Fowler
Sgt R. J. Hinchcliffe
Sgt R. J. Hussey
Sgt D. B. Leaf (American)
Sgt H. S. Lewis (American)
Sgt F. Malan
Sgt B. J. Oliver (New Zealand)
Sgt K. N. Stoker
Sgt E. L. Westly (Norwegian)
Sgt R. A. Wright

TRAINING & MORE TRAINING: AUGUST & SEPTEMBER 1942

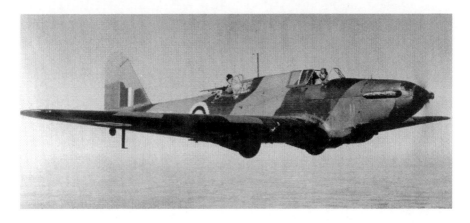

A Fairey Battle in RAF camouflage scheme. No.4 Air Gunners School at Morpeth had one of these aircraft on strength as a training machine, but it was finished in an overall yellow scheme with black diagonal stripes, as per the Lysanders that were also assigned to the unit. (Crown Copyright expired)

The summer of 1942 saw RAF Morpeth receiving a new commander when Wing Commander J. A. H. Louden arrived on the 17th from the Air Ministry. Wing Commander Jones left for No.1 Air Armament School at RAF Manby five days later, when the official handover period was completed. However, the new boss was almost immediately treated to a quick lesson in just how training units situated well away from the front lines could face tragedies of their own. Botha W5155 crashed into the sea on 18th August 1942, the day after Wing Commander Loudon arrived at Morpeth. The aircraft went down just north-east of the lifeboat station at Boulmer in Northumberland after colliding with Lysander TT Mk.III T1506's towing cable in bad weather during an air-to-air firing training sortie. The Lysander was reported as burnt out after crashlanding just inshore. There were seven crammed into the Botha: the pilot, Kapral Zgmunt Myszkowski, the wireless operator and gunnery instructor, Sgt. William Beeley, and five trainees. The lifeboat was launched and found an inflatable dinghy, a dead body and a seriously wounded airman, Leading Aircraftsman T. A. Emberson, who died shortly after being recovered from the sea. Local salvage authorities stated that it was impossible to retrieve the wreck of the Botha and the five remaining airmen from the seabed. The two crew members onboard the Lysander, the pilot, Sergeant B. Carter and the Towed Target Operator, Sergeant A. C. Dickinson, were both injured. Dickinson had received minor burns whilst extricating his pilot from the crashed Lysander, which caught fire after it crash-landed. Sergeant Carter's burns were more extensive, and he was rushed to Alnwick Infirmary. Zgmunt Myszkowski's pilot's grave can be seen today in St Mary's Churchyard, Morpeth. He had been one of a group of six pilots, including Josef Jaworzyn, who had been posted from the Polish Service Flying Training School when the School opened in May 1942.

The following day, Botha W5121 crashed at Bedlington after its starboard engine failed. There was extensive damage to the aircraft's fuselage. However, there were no casualties amongst those onboard at the time. Meanwhile, on the domestic front, the battle to secure proper sanitary arrangements across the station took a step nearer ending as officials had arrived for an inspection at the start of August 1942. They stated that connecting water and sewerage supplies to all facilities located on the Headquarters and Technical Sites would cost around £6,000, about £290,000 in today's money (2021 figures). On a happier note, the WAAFs were finally allowed into their new Communal Site as it was completed on 19th August 1942. In addition, the fifteen airmen who were being checked for air-sickness were tested again in mid-August but showed no further ill-effects.

September 1942 began with visits by Wing Commander Davies, Education Officer of Flying Training Command, plus No.29 (Training) Group's Physical Fitness Officer, Flight Lieutenant McPartlin. Both turned up on the 4th to inspect various parts of the station that fell under their respective remits. Air Commodore Norton, commander of No.29 Group, arrived by air for an inspection on the same day, accompanied by his Senior Air Staff Officer, Group Captain Brodie. It appears that everything seemed to be in order as no mention of remedial work is listed in the official records. However, Physical Fitness Officers from No.29 Group (the aforementioned McPartlin) and his opposite number from Flying Training Command arrived on the 15th, so there may well have been issues regarding personnel fitness that needed to be addressed.

On the following day, No.7 Course passed out on completion of their training, whilst the personnel that were assigned to No.11 Course arrived at RAF Morpeth. The station was now operating with no less than four courses running simultaneously, albeit at different stages of their syllabuses. No.7 Course was comprised of 60 pupils, one of which withdrew from training due to sickness. Two were killed in the crash on 18th August. There were still no camera guns for use by the School, which hampered the instructors' efforts, and this was recorded in the official log. A total of 641 flying hours were logged by the pupils, each receiving around 11 in the air. None of the trainees were recommended for retention as instructors.

A visit by Air Commodore Hewit, the Principal Medical Officer from No.29 Group, on 8th September resulted in swift action to remedy the lack of adequate ventilation in many of the station's accommodation huts. The problem was outlined as follows:

"Damp concrete floors and the consequent deterioration and in some cases partial destruction of linoleum in barrack huts is to be investigated at once."

Some accidents thankfully involved no loss of life but were still detrimental to the smooth running of the station and the training of air gunners. One of these concerned Botha W5123, which was being serviced on 13th September 1942. An engine fitter started up the aircraft's starboard engine for testing purposes without first ensuring that wheel chocks had been used to prevent the machine moving. None had been placed under the tyres, so the Botha swung around 180° and collided with a tractor, presumably a ground tug vehicle for pulling aircraft out of the hangars. The aircraft's fuselage and both tailplanes were damaged in the incident, although repairs allowed it to return to service several days later. The temporary loss of a Botha did however impact on the training programme, and the fitter was reprimanded for his negligence.

The gunners' courses continued to arrive and depart. On 19th September, No.8 Course completed their training and No.12 Course trainees arrived at Morpeth to begin theirs. The latter consisted of cadets from No.12 School of Techincal Training, RAF Hereford, who were being re-trained in the air gunner role. Again, 60 pupils made up No.8 Course, of which four failed to complete their training – three were withdrawn due to sickness whilst a fourth failed to pass. The latter was returned to the Initial Training Wing at Blackpool for reassignment, presumably into a ground trade. The lack of camera gun equipment was by that stage having an effect on the efficiency of the School. Staff at No.29 (Training Group) were clearly aware of the problem as an Air Ministry Order was made to obtain stocks for use by No.4 Air Gunners School. The better weather experienced by No.8 Course was reflected in their flying hours total – 725 hours. No pupils were recommended for commissions but three were thought suitable to undertake instructors' courses and were recommended for such duties. The accuracy scores had settled down although the air-to-air averages still gave cause for some concern. The slightly lower than hoped for figures were explained by the strict adherence to 300 yards range during all airborne gunnery practice flights, an increase in distance compared to what the first few courses at RAF Morpeth experienced. Ground training was considered acceptable but the lack of ammunition, clays and traps for shotguns meant that this section of the gunnery training was somewhat neglected.

No.9 Course was completed on the 26th and then replaced by personnel assigned to No.13, which was made up of airmen from No.14 Initial Training Wing at Bridlington, North Yorkshire. These units were not situated at airfields but at seaside resorts where there was plenty of private accommodation that could be used as temporary billets for trainee airmen. These were men newly arrived from "Civvie Street", and the units taught them the basics of being

Royal Air Force non-commissioned personnel, with testing to judge aptitude towards the different roles available in the service. Among its various sub-units, RAF Bridlington was home to an Elementary Air Gunners School, which held six week long courses on the subject although as it was not housed at an airfield or had assigned aircraft, its actual value was limited to providing trainees with a taste of what was to come at stations such as Morpeth.

Wallace McIntosh was one of the trainee air gunners who arrived at Morpeth towards the end of September 1942. His opinion of the Botha appeared much more favourable, although his affection for the type was summed up as follows:

"[It] probably originated from the excitement of scudding through the sky with Polish pilots who endeavoured to put a bit of zip into an otherwise boring job, which had become a glorified taxi service for sprog gunners."

He had even seen his first Botha before joining the course at No.4 Air Gunners School, watching it take off from Morpeth as he was driven up from the railway station in the back of a truck. According to his book, *Gunning for the Enemy*:

"[He] watched it almost lovingly (...) knowing it would be the first aeroplane that would lift him off the ground and help turn him into an air gunner. It waggled its wings, rumbled off towards the North Sea with another bunch of trainees..."

Due to all of the countries being represented at Morpeth, it was a rather cosmopolitan place, even though some of the officers were clearly from a different class. Everyone seemed to muck in together when they were needed. McIntosh reflected on this in his book:

"At Morpeth, I was with fellows who had been to public schools and university. There was a sprinkling of men who had re-mustered from other RAF trades. They all wanted to do their bit."

Warrant Officer Lawrence Casey, who was one of the instructors at No.4 Air Gunners School, RAF Morpeth. The photograph was taken before he was posted to the unit as the aircraft behind him are Lockheed Hudson light bomber and coastal reconnaissance machines, which never visited or were based at Morpeth. This looks like a posed photo. (Via David E. Clark)

Listening to some of the more experienced trainee gunners on the courses that had already started usually paid dividends for those personnel who were newly arrived at No.4 Air Gunners School. Wallace McIntosh remembered being told that he should try and be first into the dorsal turret of the Botha during the gunnery practice flights over the North Sea ranges:

"This was helpful 'gen' because it meant I avoided going into a turret full of vomit. Four or five gunners normally went up together and we took it in turns to go into the turret. Very often, a couple could not hang onto their breakfast or lunch. The smell in that aircraft was abominable and some poor bastard had to hose-pipe it down after we'd landed."

McIntosh himself had not been immune from airsickness at Morpeth:

"I wasn't a bossy boots, but I always made sure I was first to fire the Brownings, so I was in the fresh air, before going forward to sit beside the pilot for the rest of the flight and admire the view. I was very badly sick the first time I flew, but never again."

Whilst it was generally unloved, the Botha did have one advantage when it came to training gunners: the fully-hydraulic Frazer-Nash mid-upper gun turret was the same type as fitted in the twin-engined Avro Manchester Mk.I, plus very early examples of the company's more-famous four-engined Lancaster bomber. In addition, the Botha could reach 275 mph, quicker than an Avro Anson or an Airspeed Oxford, which were also used in the gunnery and multi-engine conversion training roles respectively.

Wallace McIntosh clearly had a soft spot for the Polish pilots based at Morpeth, and described them fondly, if not always favourably, in his book *Gunning for the Enemy*:

"I flew with nine different pilots at Morpeth, most of them Poles, all mad bastards, but tough guys who could really handle an aircraft. They loved to fly and were great fliers. They didn't fly with a crew, just the trainee gunners."

The madcap nature of some of the Polish airmen was evident:

"They jumped in [the aircraft] and cried out 'Come on lads, be seated.' They'd be taxiing down the runway before the door was closed."

Once the gunnery training detail was over, the Poles seemed to relish the opportunity to fly low and fast over the local countryside, terrifying the lives of locals:

"They didn't want to be hanging about up there and often said 'Get the bloody firing over bloody quick, then we go for a ride.' So we'd fire off our rounds and go hare-assing across the sea, beat up Morpeth and Alnwick, dart up the Northumbrian moors, along the Borders over the hills and heather, starting at 200 feet then going right down on the deck."

It was small wonder that more airmen were not sick in the back of the Botha. The low-level beat-ups of local towns and farms at high speed were accompanied by commentaries from the pilots, telling the trainees what speed and altitude they were flying at, describing the scenery and checking everyone was still feeling fine. The Poles were equally concerned about the trainees throwing up in their Bothas, but often just made a joke about it:

"'Come on boys," they would say. 'Own up, who's been sick in the bottom of my aeroplane today? Do it in your battledress, but don't leave it in the aircraft. I don't mind you leaving money or fags, but not sick."

Gunnery practice and the low-level flying comprised the exciting parts of the training syllabus, but more mundane, yet equally as important were the ground lectures on aircraft recognition. No-one wanted to see the air gunners shooting down their own side. Every training day featured at least an hour's recognition, which usually saw silhouettes of the normal *Luftwaffe* night-fighter force being featured, along with some pitfalls in the shape of Bristol Blenheims, which at a glance could be mistaken for the Junkers Ju 88 due to their similarities – both had twin engines and a single tail fin.

No.9 Course completed their training on 25th September 1942, with just 53 of the pupils passing – the lowest number so far. Two airmen had failed the course, four were suspended and another was withdrawn due to sickness. At least two of the above found themselves returned to Blackpool for reassignment. The number of total flying hours dropped to 668. The reduced pass rate warranted a mention in the No.4 Air Gunners School official records:

"The discipline and general behaviour of this intake was below the standard set by previous courses. Progressive examination results were not satisfactory. 4 cadets were suspended from further training, being considered unsuitable in every respect. This action had an improving effect on the remainder of the course, only two cadets failing to pass the final examination."

Consequently, none of the cadets were recommended for retention as instructors or to receive commissions. A new addition to the various types of synthetic gunnery training equipment was a Royal Aircraft Establishment Tracer Trainer, which featured a moveable silhouette and spotlight. Gunners could track a "moving target" with dummy guns, although there was supposed to be a film projected onto the wall where the silhouette moved. This was absent, pending the arrival of a film unit which had yet to arrive at RAF Morpeth. The cadets on No.9 Course did at least receive live dinghy drill training, being taken to an indoor swimming pool across at Ashington.

The posting of Leading Aircraftsman G. R. Hartley from No.4 Air Gunners School to RAF Padgate on the 27th for overseas duty may not on the face of it seem very important, but it caused a problem for the unit at the end of the month. Hartley was the Amble Range's Medical Orderly, and his posting left the sub-unit without a suitably trained airman. The detachment therefore had to operate without one as there was an acute shortage of medical personnel at RAF Morpeth. The situation was eventually resolved by No.29 (Training)

Group's Senior Medical Officer liaising with his opposite number at No.13 (Fighter) Group Headquarters in Newcastle. The outcome of these negotiations was that medical staff at RAF Acklington, which was much closer to Amble than Morpeth, would be responsible for the treatment and "disposal" of airmen detached there from the Air Gunners School.

September's statistics were impressive: 610 flying hours carried out by the School's Bothas, plus a further 499 by its Lysander target tugs. Even the single Fairey Battle assigned to the unit as a training aircraft managed seven hours' flying time during the month, the machine providing tug pilots with a useful means of honing their skills without having to use one of the valuable Lysanders, all of which were needed for the busy training schedule. Some 327,650 rounds were fired in air-to-air practice training, plus 146,450 at the ground firing butts.

FURTHER MISHAPS: OCTOBER-DECEMBER 1942

A Miles Master advanced training aircraft. No.4 Air Gunners School acquired at least one of these machines by November 1942. Several examples were later used by No.80 (French) Operational Training Unit at Morpeth in 1945. As fast as the biplanes that had seen front-line service before the arrival of Hurricanes and Spitfires, the Master included modern features such as a fully-enclosed cockpit, retractable undercarriage and in some examples, a single machine gun fitted into each wing. It was an ideal lead-in trainer for pilots who had trained on Tiger Moth biplanes and were destined to fly high performance aircraft. The examples at Morpeth gave staff pilots the chance to train without having to use the Lysander aircraft that were fully engaged in target towing flights. (Crown Copyright expired)

October 1942 did not start well for No.4 Air Gunners School. On the 1st, Botha W5142 sank into soft ground whilst taxying out onto the perimeter track at Morpeth. Damage was sustained to the aircraft's port undercarriage unit, although the machine was later repaired. The pilot, Sergeant G. R. Jackson, a New Zealander, was subjected to a Court of Inquiry ordered by the Air Officer Commanding, No.29 (Training Group). Sergeant Jackson was allowed to continue flying but we will encounter his name again, notably in March 1943.

On the same day, Westland Lysander T1521, flown by Sergeant W. Shepherd, force-landed up at RAF Eshott. After a morning spent towing target drogues over the Druridge Bay ranges, he had landed at Acklington for fuel and lunch. When departing the aerodrome, Shepherd found that the aircraft's engine was misfiring badly, and in addition it was losing power. Eshott was only a couple of miles to the west of Acklington, and so the pilot elected to put the Lysander down there before matters worsened. The aircraft was examined, and a report issued, a summary of which was included in the official No.4 Air Gunners School file:

"An examination of the carburettor and subsequent engine test revealed that petrol was accumulating in the automatic control chamber, thereby rendering this control inoperative."

It was just as well that RAF Acklington had been ordered to assume responsibility for the medical needs of the No.4 Air Gunners School personnel at Amble. On 3rd October, Aircraftsman Houston fell while on duty, fracturing his skull. An investigation was carried out to try and determine the cause of the incident.

No.10 (Straight) Air Gunners Course passed out after completing their training on the 10th and were replaced at Morpeth by No.14 (Straight) Course. 63 cadets made up the course, and just a single pupil failed to complete it successfully, having been suspended after the first progressive examination. A further three had to leave due to sickness. One of the successful cadets was recommended for a commission. Compared with the previous course, discipline was said to be good, and the average scores compared favourably with the best of the early intakes.

A new piece of equipment known as the "Johnson Shadowgraph" had also been installed to assist the trainee gunners in determining the range of targets. This could train several gunners simultaneously in aircraft recognition. A silhouette of an aircraft model was projected onto a screen, in front of which two or three long benches capable of seating a dozen or more pupils could be positioned. The Shadowgraph was therefore a quick and relatively inexpensive synthetic training device.

Personnel from RAF Morpeth were increasingly being required to attend crash sites involving aircraft belonging to other units, due to the lack of suitably-trained staff within the local area. Although No.83 Maintenance Unit at Woolsington were supposed to deal with such incidents, they were stretched incredibly thin due to the huge area that the unit had been assigned to cover. Due to an ever-increasing number of incidents across Northumberland, Durham and Cumberland, it was inevitable that other RAF units in these areas would be called upon to either assist the Maintenance Unit or stand in for them. One such incident occurred on 13th October, when Hurricane Mk.I P3524 from No.59 Operational Training Unit up at Milfield, near Wooler, force-landed in a field at Netherwitton, about eight miles north-west of RAF Morpeth. The aircraft had suffered a severe internal Glycol leak, the lack of engine coolant resulting in a complete engine malfunction. The Hurricane was damaged in the force landing and classified as "Category B", i.e. beyond repair on site. The aircraft was dismantled and taken away for examination and repair.

On 17th October, No.11 (Straight) Course passed out and was replaced by No.15 Course. 61 pupils had begun No.11 Course, one of whom failed the final exam. One cadet was recommended for a commission and two to attend Air Gunner Instructor courses at RAF Manby. Once again, it was remarked in official records that the course was slightly below previously-attained standards in terms of results and discipline, although periods of bad weather had ensured that the average gunnery scores were down. Ground tracer training sessions were put on at short notice to give the gunners some sort of useful practice when the weather was too poor to fly. There was still no cine-gun camera equipment at the station. The bad weather during September and October had reduced the amount of flying hours amassed by the course to just 606, which meant that each cadet had just over 10 hours to obtain as much air-to-air practice as possible before being assigned to a crew.

A larger-than-normal contingent of senior staff personnel turned up at Morpeth for an inspection on 20th October. Air Commodore Thomas, Senior Air Staff Officer, Flying Training Command, was accompanied by Lieutenant Colonel Barratt, No.29 (Training) Group Defence Officer, Squadron Leader Bibby, No.29 Group Air Staff Officer, Squadron Leader Vaughan, Flying Training Command's Gas Officer and his opposite number at No.29 Group, Flight Lieutenant Wrightson. They stayed overnight and departed on the 21st.

A further senior staff visit saw Wing Commander Green and Flight Lieutenant Cunningham from No.29 (Training) Group being accompanied by Flight Lieutenant R. M. Shaw, Flying Training Command's Catering Officer on the 27th. It is not clear what the purpose of the visit was, but the inclusion of a catering officer would lead one to suggest the various Mess buildings were inspected.

Wing Commander Loudon was joined on the 27th by Wing Commander J. D. Nelson, who had been posted to RAF Morpeth on a temporary attachment basis from Manby in Lincolnshire, pending his assignment to a new station. His time in Northumberland was certainly temporary, as three days later he was posted to RAF Mona on Anglesey, which was due to house No.3 Air Gunners School that was transferring from Castle Kennedy near Stranraer in December. Wing Commander Nelson's brief time at Morpeth would therefore have given him some idea of the problems faced by units operating the Botha in the air gunnery training role. His new unit had around fifty of these aircraft on strength.

October 1942 ended with the passing of both No.12 and No.13 Courses on the same day, the 31st. With the increased number of pupils in each intake, it appears a decision was taken to reduce the courses at Morpeth to three at any one time. No.16 Course arrived on the same day. The total flying hours for the month was recorded as 702 for the Botha fleet and 448 for the Lysander Mk.I target tugs, plus another 78 for the Mk.IIIs. Another nine hours were notched up using the Battle, again presumably for pilot training.

A group photograph taken of No.12 Course at Morpeth in October 1942. Sturgess Herbert Rayner is second bottom row, second from right. (Via Christina Spencer)

November 1942 began with a change of Senior Medical Officer, due to Flight Lieutenant Page receiving notice of a posting overseas. He was replaced on the 3rd by Flight Lieutenant Maclure. A check of the medical equipment inventory revealed only one deficiency, a complete lack of Spencer Wells type forceps.

In a change from the usual process, No.17 Course arrived on the 7th, a week before No.14 Course had completed its training. Things returned to normal when No.18 Course arrived on the 14th as well, the station reverting to the usual four courses running at any one time schedule. With around 250 pupils at RAF Morpeth each day, it was certainly a busy place, but the needs of Bomber Command ensured that this pace could not slacken. No.14 Course, comprised of 61 cadets, saw three of this number withdrawn before the final exams. Two of the successful trainee gunners were recommended for commissions. Work on completing a 200 yard-long ground firing range had only been completed in November 1942 and therefore No.14 Course was only able to use it right at the end of their time at Morpeth. Aircraft unserviceability and periods of bad weather also hampered the cadets' progress, although cine-gun cameras finally arrived at the School and were quickly put to good use. In addition, two RAF Night Vision Trainers were installed.

However, No.14 (Straight) Course was memorable for another reason. The usual six week-long course had been curtailed by one week on instructions received by the Air Ministry. This was due to the pressing requirements of Bomber Command, which urgently needed air gunners to replace losses in combat, plus those airmen who had completed their "tours" of missions and were transferred to instructor and other ground-based roles. The total number of flying hours for the course was therefore reduced to just 558.

The School would also lose more aircraft before 1942 was out. One of these was Botha Mk.I W5139, whose pilot, Sergeant. J. Zalenski, attempted to take off using the wrong runway on 16th November 1942. The Polish pilot collided with Botha L6339 at the intersection between two of the runways, the second aircraft being flown by Sergeant. J. Moszoro. Leading Aircraftsman John Wignall, one of the pupils aboard Zalenski's aircraft, died of his injuries in the ambulance on the way to Station Sick Quarters. Another of the cadets, Leading Aircraftman Skinner, was found to be suffering from shock but no obvious injuries and soon made a full recovery. It was declared a miracle that no more casualties were sustained, given the serious nature of the collision. Neither aircraft had caught fire.

A Board of Inquiry was ordered by No.29 (Training) Group, this being convened by Group Captain C. J. Giles, who flew in from RAF Walney, Barrow-in-Furness, the following day. A Court of Inquiry was held at Morpeth on 18th November. Its findings blamed Sergeant Zalenski for the accident, noting the following:

"[That he had] failed to (1) observe and note the runway indicator board in order to ascertain runway in use, (2) observe accurately the direction of the wind, and (3) observe whether fire engine and ambulance were in the position required for the incorrect runway he used."

A verdict of culpable negligence was issued and both aircraft were declared as completely written off. On the 20th, a Court Martial assembled at Morpeth under the presidency of Wing Commander J. M. Lissett. Three airmen were charged for various offences against RAF regulations, one of whom was Sergeant Jaworski, who was accused of low flying without permission. The charges against the Polish pilot were dismissed.

The Botha fleet at Morpeth during November 1942 only amassed a total of 585 flying hours, together with 103 by the three different variants of Lysander in use by No.4 Air Gunners School. The month also saw the end of the Lysander target tugs at Morpeth. The surviving aircraft were transferred to other units, being replaced by deliveries of brand-new Miles Martinet target tugs, the first purpose-built type to be operated by the RAF. 427 hours had been notched up by these new aircraft during November at Morpeth. Three Lysanders had been lost whilst serving with No.4 Air Gunners School and a fourth was badly damaged but repaired. Despite being converted to the role, the faithful "Lizzies" had proved to be up to the task, the 28 or so examples based at Morpeth amassing over 2,500 flying hours in total. The School had also acquired at least one Miles Master and a de Havilland Moth Minor by this stage, with the former being a training aircraft similar to the Martinet and the latter probably being a "hack" for use by Wing Commander Louden. The Moth Minor only recorded eight flying hours during the month of November. To give some idea of how much petrol all of the station's aircraft consumed, 47,040 gallons of fuel were used during November 1942.

One of the newly-arrived Martinets was lost only a few weeks after arriving at Morpeth. The Operations Record Book for No.4 Air Gunners School recorded the following for 5th December 1942:

"Martinet HN941 force-landed in sea off Amble, due to engine failure. Towed Target Operator, 1088475 A.C. Sutcliffe, died as a result of drowning and shock. Pilot, 1266012 Sgt. Jones, uninjured. A Court of Inquiry has been held to investigate the circumstances of this accident."

The RAF Morpeth Station Sick Quarters report gave more details about the incident:

"A Target Towing Aircraft (Martinet) crashed into the sea off Amble. It was piloted by 1266012 Sgt. Jones N.L. who survived and was unhurt. The Towed Target Operator 108475 L.A.C. Sutcliffe was killed. Death due to drowning and primary shock. Both men were taken to Amble Military Hospital. The body of L.A.C. Sutcliffe was brought over to RAF Morpeth 5.12.42. Sgt Jones was retained overnight at Amble owing to lack of dry clothing."

Leading Aircraftsman Sutcliffe, 22 years of age and from Bamford, Rochdale, had only been in the RAF for eighteen months. His military funeral took place at St. Michael's Church in Bamford, where he had been part of the choir for fifteen years.

On the same day, No.15 Course passed out on completion of their training, whilst the cadets assigned to No.19 Course arrived at the station. Chances are they would have heard about the Martinet crash at some stage, a rude awakening about the dangers that were faced by training units nowhere near enemy territory. No.15 Course had started off with 61 pupils, now the standard number, but one, John Wignall, had been killed in the accident on 16th November and another was withdrawn before the end of the syllabus. Just one cadet was recommended for a commission. Despite the station now having the necessary cine-gun camera equipment, the minimum number of hours of air-to-air exercises had not been reached. This would have been due to the poor flying conditions and the fact that the equipment only arrived at Morpeth after No.15 Course began. In a change to normal practice, the Air Ministry ordered that half of the cadets – 30 in total – were posted to their training crews a full week before the end of their course, whilst the remainder saw out the full term of the now-extended seven week long period of air gunnery training. Shortening the syllabus to just five weeks clearly had not produced the desired results and may have only served to produce more gunners with deficits in their training.

A strange event occurred on the 16th when Leading Aircraftsman Sawyer, who had been attached to RAF Morpeth on compassionate grounds (possibly due to family members who lived in the area), was arrested and removed by the local civilian police force. He was returned to the station a fortnight later, after a short period of incarceration. However, this was not the end of the story, as on 26th January 1943, Sawyer was sentenced at Lancaster Assizes Court to 15 months imprisonment for perjury and procuration. He had served at Barrow but was attached to Morpeth pending trial, possibly due to whatever offences he had committed at his home base.

19th December 1942 saw No.16 Course complete its training syllabus, being replaced at Morpeth by the personnel of No.20 Course. The orders received from the Air Ministry to shorten the length of the courses was soon noticeable as just three days later, No.17 Course also passed out, with No.21 Course arriving the same day. December 1942 had seen plenty of bad weather, including plenty of thick haze, with no less than 11 days being regarded as completely unfit for flying. Indeed, the No.4 Air Gunners School records state that less than 100 hours that month had been classed as "fit flying hours". The fleet of Bothas therefore only managed to fly 341 hours in total, and the target towing Martinets amassed less than 200 – all of these hours crammed into the small amount of "fit flying hours" that were available. The skies above the airfield must therefore have been very busy when conditions allowed, and it is amazing that further incidents did not occur.

No.17 Course had seen 60 cadets arrive at Morpeth, with their training beginning on 8th November 1942. This was probably the worst group yet in terms of the percentage that did not successfully pass the training course. Four airmen were withdrawn and another five failed the final exams. No commission recommendations were made.

19th December 1942 also saw an inspection at Morpeth by Wing Commander H. P. Ruffell Smith from Flying Training Command, who enquired about the welfare arrangements for both the station's personnel and the cadets from the various courses. The main objects of his inspection were the accommodation sites, the quality of the food on offer and the state of the dining rooms. Pat Ruffell Smith went onto become head of the aviation section of the RAF Institute of Flight Medicine at Farnborough, only retiring from the service in 1961. He later worked at the Ames Research Center in California, carrying out a simulator study for NASA into the *"interaction of pilot workload with errors, vigilance and decisions"*. He was also a consultant to British Airways and British Leyland.

A NEW YEAR DAWNS: JANUARY-MARCH 1943

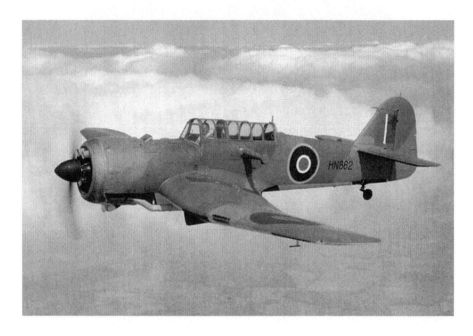

Martinet TT Mk.I HN862 served with an Anti-Aircraft Co-Operation Flight in East Yorkshire before being lost in a crash in July 1943. It is identical to the target towing Martinets that served with No.4 Air Gunners School at RAF Morpeth. Note the fixed bar protruding from below the cockpit canopy, part of the aircraft's towing apparatus. (Crown Copyright expired)

January 1943 began with No.18 Course passing out on the 2nd and No.22 Course arriving at Morpeth for the start of their own training. No.18 started with 62 cadets, the largest group yet, Three of these failed the course, which ran smoothly for a change, although there was a complete lack of clays for the shotgun practice. Squadron Leader Bibby at No.29 (Training) Group Headquarters was informed of the situation and promised to take action. Some 521 flying hours were amassed by No.18 Course although the average per pupil was way down on previous intakes, with just 8 hours being flown by each trainee. This meant that the successful candidates had not received much air-to-air firing practice, largely due to the conditions experienced in December 1942.

January 1943 seemed to be a quiet affair, although an incident that occurred on the 24th marred an otherwise perfect month in terms of accidents. The official No.4 Air Gunners School records take up the story:

"Martinet aircraft Nos. HB132 and HN910 involved in taxying accident causing damage to both aircraft. Martinet HN910 was being taxyed [sic] from dispersal to blister hanger when brakes failed. The aircraft continued to run down a slope and collided with Martinet HB132."

No-one was injured in the incident. Both aircraft were repaired and returned to service.

The large Polish contingent among the regular flying staff at RAF Morpeth were treated to a visit by two of their countrymen on the 26th, with both Squadron Leader Jan Bialy and Squadron Leader Peszke arriving from No.29 (Training) Group. They were the senior Polish officers from the Group's headquarters. Jan Bialy reportedly hated "flying a desk" and soon requested a return to combat duties, which he was granted later in January 1943. He therefore became the oldest active pilot in the Polish Air Force stationed in Britain, as he was 46 years old at the time. Moving to Italy in 1944, Bialy took part in a special operation which saw him parachuting into Poland to assume command of a Home Army detachment near Lublin. He was captured and imprisoned by the Russians but released after the end of the war in Europe, although he was arrested again by the secret police in 1952 and put in prison for several months – an experience shared by many former Polish and Czech airmen who had returned home after serving in the RAF during the war.

On 30th January, Morpeth received an official visit from Air Commodore H. A. Hewat, Principal Medical Officer of Flying Training Command. He inspected Sites No.1 and No.6, and then visited the WAAF Sites, paying particular attention to their sick quarters building which was still not yet ready for occupation. With the station having been operational for over nine months, this was an unacceptable state of affairs, and Harry Hewat's actions are recorded in the official No.4 Air Gunners School records:

"He instructed the Clerk of Works to hasten the completion of this building, and to take action over the lino floor covering of Station Sick Quarters and the adjoining billets were also inspected."

2nd February 1943 saw Wing Commander Lissett from No.4 (Bomber) Group Headquarters arrive to preside over the District Court Martial of Sergeant Zalenski. This followed on from the Board of Inquiry which took place two days after the fateful ground collision on 16th November 1942 where an airman died. Zalenski had already been found to be at fault for the incident and his fate was being decided by the Court Martial.

On the same day, one of No.4 Air Gunners School's Martinets (serial unknown but wearing the code "25") was involved in an accident at Morpeth. Sergeant Sears was at the controls, when the aircraft swung and then ran off the runway whilst he was taking off. Sears was uninjured but checked out at Station Sick Quarters as a precaution.

A flurry of staff visits during the first half of the month included Wing Commander Cameron, Senior Medical Officer from No.29 Group on the 8th. He was interested in learning whether the medical arrangements of RAF Morpeth and RAF Stannington could be combined, the latter facility being located just a mile east of the aerodrome. This arrangement appeared to make sense, especially given the admitted lack of medical personnel assigned to Morpeth. Using Stannington's medical staff was one solution although it would mean a larger overall number of personnel that a combined Sick Quarters had responsibility for, who were spread out over a much wider area.

Two members of the Air Ministry turned up on the 11th and the Air Officer Commanding No.29 Group, Air Commodore Norton, arrived on the 16th. The latter was interested in learning about the general health of personnel assigned to RAF Morpeth and wanted to know more about the incidents of venereal disease that had been reported by personnel there. Squadron Leader Nicholls was posted to Morpeth on the 10th as Officer Commanding, Flying. He arrived from No.5 Air Observers School at Jurby, situated at the northern (and flat) end of the Isle of Man. His job was to oversee all aspects of the flying programme.

No.19 Course completed their training on 6th February and were immediately replaced by No.23 Course. No.19 had begun with the regular figure of 60 pupils, three of whom failed to pass the course. However, three more were recommended for commissions and another trio retained at Morpeth as instructors. It was not unusual for some of the best trainee gunners to be held back from front-line duties, especially if they had demonstrated an aptitude for passing on what they had learned to their colleagues whilst undertaking the course. Some would eventually elect to move onto a squadron, but others stayed at the School, preferring to train the new batches of airmen passing through the station. A shortage of cine-gun cameras was again affecting training, however, and eight of these had to be loaned from No.10 Air Gunners School at RAF Walney, near Barrow in Furness.

Records were now being kept regarding the number of hours on average trainees spent using the ground turrets on the firing ranges. Each had about 12 hours in these to start with, in order to familiarise themselves with a gun turret's operation before they started air-to-air firing practice. The Fraser-Nash turrets used in ground drills were somewhat similar to those fitted to the bomber aircraft the successful trainees would end up in once they joined an operational squadron, although newer ones were starting to reach the front-line units. A few turrets were installed inside buildings for initial instruction and synthetic training, but others were fixed onto open-bed trucks for use at the firing butts, although the latter structures were sited so that Bothas could be parked in position and their own turrets used. Whatever the method used, RAF Morpeth would have been an extremely noisy place with the almost continuous sound of machine gun fire reverberating across the aerodrome and the surrounding area.

On 20th February, No.20 Course passed out, its personnel being replaced by the new intake of No.24 Course. Arguably the most important visitor of the month was Marshall of the Royal Air Force, The Viscount Trenchard, G. C. B., G. C. V. C., D. S. O., D. C. L., LL. D., who arrived at Morpeth by air on the 27th. He stayed overnight with his staff contingent and carried out an official inspection of the station the following day, lecturing cadets and leaving later in the afternoon by road.

The total of flying hours in February 1943 was again down on the highs of the previous year, no doubt due to bad weather, although it was a vast improvement over the last two months. The Botha fleet managed to fly 553 hours and the Martinets 465. The single Miles Master Mk.II operated by the School was flown for just seven hours during the month, probably for pilot training purposes. Some 209,100 rounds of 0.303-inch ammunition was used in air-to-air firing exercises, plus another 224,800 on the ground firing ranges. One can imagine the stocks of bullets that were constantly needed by the School, an important commodity which could not be allowed to run out.

No.22 Course passed out on 6th March. 61 pupils began training on 3rd January 1943, but one airman was soon withdrawn at his own request. Four more were transferred from the School before they could complete the course and another five failed the final exam. This led to the worst success rate so far. None of the intake were retained as instructors. The pupils had only averaged eight hours in ground turret training.

Another accident occurred on 8th March 1943 when a Botha aircraft (which was identified in the official log as "N.561") crashed on take-off. It failed to rise from the runway and struck a lorry. There were thankfully no injuries to any of the crew or trainees onboard. The aircraft involved in this incident was Botha Mk.I W5164, and other accounts suggest it hit either a tree or a trolley. The following day, an ambulance was summoned to the aerodrome as a petrol bowser vehicle overturned. No casualties resulted from the accident.

A preserved de Havilland DH.94 Moth Minor in New Zealand. A similar aircraft was used at Morpeth as a personal "hack" by Wing Commander (later Group Captain) Louden, the station's commanding officer. Note the open cockpit. (Phil Vabre, via free GNU documentation licence)

A specialist orthoptist arrived on 16th March to test the night vision of cadets from the various courses who had yet to be tested. Clearly this was an important issue, and many of those withdrawn from previous courses may have been picked up in screening such as this.

Another aircraft was damaged on 17th March when Botha Mk.I W5140 was involved in a take-off incident. Flight Sergeant Jones was at the controls for an air test and had no other crew or pupils onboard at the time. A tyre burst as he rolled down the runway, causing the machine to swing to one side and run off the tarmac. The propeller blades and undercarriage units sustained damage, but the aircraft was eventually repaired.

On 24th March, Wing Commander Godson, Royal Canadian Air Force, paid a visit to Morpeth, liaising with senior staff officers for training purposes. Although No.4 Air Gunners School is associated with Polish airmen, it should not be forgotten that personnel from most if not all of the Commonwealth countries served at the station, including several Canadians. Wing Commander Wyatt from the Air Ministry also attended on the same day as part of an Allied Liaison Visit. They were followed the next day by Wing Commander Bruce from the Air Ministry and Squadron Leader Hugh from No.29 Group and then Flight Lieutenant Tegner, a member of the Ministry of Aircraft Production. Wing Commander Godson stayed for three days and then flew to Dalcross (now Inverness Airport) for another engagement.

No.23 Course passed out on 27th March. The pass rate was much improved on the previous intake, with 60 out of an original 64 trainees completing the course successfully, although three were withdrawn at their own request. The selection process for potential gunners may not have weeded out all of those cadets who ended up being unsuitable for aircrew positions. Unfavourable weather hit the last week of the course, affecting the training. Just nine hours on average were spent using the ground turret trainers.

Flying hours for March totalled 527 hours 45 minutes for the Botha aircraft and 416 hours 50 minutes for the Martinet fleet. A few more hours were put in for pilot training using the Master, but the station's Moth Minor was hardly used, being flown for just two hours 40 minutes in total during March 1943. The total amount of ammunition expended was also down, with 237,000 rounds being used in air training and just 149,000 in ground instruction.

TRAGEDY OVER MORPETH: MARCH 1943

Two Botha aircraft Nos. W5154 and W5137 collided in mid air and resulted in the death of two officers and seven other ranks.

The short entry in the No.4 Air Gunners School records marking the mid-air collision involving two Botha aircraft over Morpeth in March 1943.

The tragic incident that occurred at RAF Morpeth on 29th March 1943 became a permanent fixture in the memory of all who witnessed it. Jack Thompson, a local resident at the time, witnessed what happened that day:

"I was cycling from Pegswood to Morpeth on 29th March 1943 when I witnessed a mid-air collision between Bothas W5137 and W5154 in the circuit. One went straight in at 45 degrees, and the other flew for a few more seconds enabling one crewmember to bail out, but his 'chute only streamed. All nine crewmen were killed, including Major Zarski, the senior Polish pilot at Morpeth, aged 46. The other pilot was Pilot Officer G. R. Jackson, Royal New Zealand Air Force. Five of the two crews were Dutch, the youngest only 18, and there were 2 RAF crew. I visited the scene with a lad whose father was a doctor at the Gateshead Mental Hospital, Stannington. (This was St. Mary's, the former Gateshead Borough Asylum.) Most of the wreckage had been cleared away but there were lots of bits and pieces, and unfortunately, small scraps of flesh and bone ail over the place."

Air Vice Marshal Sir Philip Babington was visiting RAF Morpeth that day and a demonstration of the School's aircraft had been laid on for his benefit. The visit had already been postponed as he had originally intended to inspect the station on 17th March. He was accompanied by the Air Office Commanding, No.29 Group, Air Commodore Norton, plus Group Captain Cyril Heard from Flying

Training Command Headquarters. As Officer Commanding in Chief, Flying Training Command, the Air Vice Marshall was in charge of all the of Air Gunners Schools located across Britain. Also visiting the station on the same day were Wing Commander Krzyczkowski and Squadron Leader Peszke, who enquired into the general health and wellbeing of Polish personnel at Morpeth. The weather should have precluded any flying display, since none of the normal training flights were taking place due to the poor weather conditions, but the demonstration was apparently insisted upon in any case.

The 58 members of No.24 Course pictured here include 15 members of the Royal Netherlands Naval Air Service. Daniel Kooij is front row, second left, Arie van Egmond is fourth in line, Bernardus van Opdorp is standing on the extreme right, Frans van Westenbrugge is front row, fifth from right, whilst Rudi van den Bron is third from right. All five were killed in the mid-air collision that took place at RAF Morpeth on 29th March 1943. Leading Aircraftsman Frank Beresford, who was also killed in the incident, is pictured at the top left of the photo.

A couple of Bothas were ordered to take off and lay on a performance. The first was W5137 (coded "14"), flown by Flight

Lieutenant S. Z. Zarski, who at 46 years of age was easily the most senior of the Polish pilots at Morpeth. Onboard his aircraft were three trainees from No.24 Course who had almost finished their training, Leading Aircraftsman Frank Beresford, *Matroos* Daniel Kooij and *Matroos* Frans van Westenbrugge. A fifth airman was also apparently onboard, Aircraftsman Tomasz Rzeznikiewicz. He was a member of Replacement Bureau No.1 Holding Unit (Poland). Rzeznikiewicz's name does not always feature when this incident is mentioned in books or on websites.

The second aircraft involved in the incident was W5154 (coded "10"), flown by Pilot Officer George Jackson, a 22 year-old New Zealander. He was carrying Sergeant Edward Hall, an instructor, and three Dutch trainees, *Vliegtuigmaker* Rudi van den Bron (the eighteen year-old), *Matroos* Arie van Egmond and *Matroos* Bernardus van Opdorp. The five Dutch trainee air gunners were all members of the Royal Netherlands Naval Air Service. Pilot Officer Jackson took off from Morpeth and climbed away successfully. Five minutes later, at 1145 hours, he collided with Zarski's Botha at a height of around 1,200 feet whilst in the circuit, about two miles east of the aerodrome. Both aircraft appeared to be returning to Morpeth at the time. The machines crashed some ¾ mile east of RAF Stannington.

All ten airmen onboard perished, one of the Bothas diving straight into the ground. The other went into a shallower dive, with witnesses remembering seeing one of the airmen in this aircraft attempting to parachute to safety after the collision. Unfortunately, his 'chute did not open correctly and he was killed. According to the medical staff at the aerodrome, death had been instantaneous and all of the recovered bodies and remains were brought to the station for examination and burial.

According to a fellow airman who was at the funeral held at St Mary's Churchyard in Morpeth, the funeral was well attended:

"The entire town seemed to be there. Everyone was moved by the circumstances of their death."

One of the Dutch gunnery trainees killed in the mid-air collision on 29th March 1943 was Matroos Danial Kooij, a 23-year-old serving with the Royal Netherlands Naval Air Service. His grave can be found at St. Mary's Churchyard, Morpeth.

The graves of many of the dead can be still seen at the rear of the churchyard itself, along with other casualties from No.4 Air Gunners School and numerous servicemen who died from tuberculosis in the Polish Resettlement Corps after the war.

Flight Lieutenant S. Z. Zarski was the pilot of Botha W5137/14 which was involved in the mid-air collision at Morpeth on 29th March 1943. He was an experienced pilot and possibly the oldest operational pilot serving with No.4 Air Gunners School as he was 46 years old at the time of his death. As with Danial Kooij, Zarski's grave can be found at St. Mary's Churchyard in Morpeth. (Author)

Pilot Officer G. R. Jackson was the pilot of W5154, the other Blackburn Botha aircraft involved in the mid-air collision in March 1943. According to the subsequent investigation, both pilots were blamed for not keeping an adequate look out for other aircraft in the landing circuit at RAF Morpeth. (Author)

Mention of the incident in the official No.4 Air Gunners School records is confined to just two lines:

"Two Botha aircraft Nos. W5154 and W5137 collided in mid-air and resulted in the death of two officers and seven other ranks."

However, the official RAF Form 1180 accident card for Botha Mk.I W5154 lists the following additional details:

"A/C collide in circuit at 1,200 ft & crash [unreadable] - pilot probably dived away to avoid collision but without success. OC [Officer Commanding] No evidence re cause or responsibility as yet."

A later addition to the same document was more forthcoming:

"Failure of both pilots to maintain adequate lookout. P/O Jackson carries greater share of blame."

The incident that day in March 1943 was one of the worst mid-air collisions to have ever occurred in Northumberland. Despite the loss of two aircraft and ten airmen, seemingly nothing was done about the lack of discipline in the circuit at Morpeth until February 1944.

NEW "KIT": APRIL-JUNE 1943

A footpath in the woods? No, it is one of the concrete roads through the former technical site at RAF Morpeth, now long since overgrown. (Author)

The first week of April 1943 saw funerals for the airmen who were killed in the mid-air collision at the end of March. Flight Lieutenant Zarski was laid to rest at St. Mary's on 2nd April and the other seven (excluding Aircraftsman Tomasz Rzeznikiewicz, whose name does not appear in the official records) the following day.

Unconnected with the tragedy but possibly welcomed by the more religious personnel serving at Morpeth was the visit of the Right Reverend Noel Hudson, the Lord Bishop of Newcastle, who was the guest of the Mess on 3rd and 4th April 1943. He was there to administer the Rite of Confirmation at the Parade Service to one WAAF officer, six WAAF other ranks and one airman. Four of the WAAFs were based at Stannington. When the Lord Bishop's visit had originally been arranged, there were at least 20 candidates for the Rite of Confirmation, but most had been posted overseas in the intervening period. Those present were excused duty so that they could attend Communion and then have breakfast with the Lord Bishop in the Corporals' NAAFI.

Meanwhile, Wing Commander Louden, the Commanding Officer of RAF Morpeth had been promoted to Group Captain. He was absent from the station from 3rd-5th April as he was visited Flying Training Command, presumably to personally inform senior officers about the progress being made at Morpeth. In his absence, Squadron Leader L. A. Simpson assumed command of the station.

6th April 1943 saw two Airwomen Flight Mechanics arriving at Morpeth, the first of many female fitters to be employed by No.4 Air Gunners School. Ensuring competence across all ground trades was vital, and the first Local Trade Test Board was held on the 8th with at least 50 airmen candidates from a wide variety of positions across the station being examined.

Three days later, the Lord Bishop of Whitby, the Right Reverend Harold Hubbard, paid an eleven day long visit to Morpeth and Stannington. He was one of several clergymen seconded to the RAF for a year by the Archbishops of Canterbury and York. His duties whilst visiting Morpeth were summarised in the official records:

"...visited the Station from 9th to 19th, staying in the Mess till the 15th, and afterwards at RAF Stannington. He preached at Parade Services on both Sundays, baptising three infants, including the daughter of the Commandant of Stannington, at a largely attended Baptism on April 11th. On weekdays he carried out a comprehensive tour of the Station, speaking to groups of from 4 to 204, including the Officers and Sergeants Messes and the WAAF on the subject of 'True Religion'. He spoke to the Cadets and visited them in their huts. The visit appeared to be much appreciated and to arouse a good deal of discussion on the Christian Faith and the part RAF personnel can play as individuals in furthering God's purpose in the world. The Bishop was asked by the COs of both Stations to pay a return visit as his stay was too short to meet the needs of two Stations adequately."

9th April 1943 saw two new Martinet aircraft being delivered to the station. Both of these sported experimental paint finishes on their wing surfaces and were the initial machines from a batch of ten such airframes selected for the purpose. The new finish was to be trialled at Morpeth, the testing expected to last six months. Two more Martinets arrived a week later.

No.24 Course completed its training on 10th April and passed out. 60 pupils had been posted to Morpeth, of which six were killed in the mid-air collision at the end of March. A further airman was withdrawn at his own request, and another thrown off the course due to being regarded as unsuitable.

A new Senior Medical Officer was appointed to Morpeth on 12th April 1943. Squadron Leader T. A. Hudson reported for duty on that day, having travelled the extremely short distance from Stannington which could probably have been accomplished on foot!

No.25 Course ended on 17th April and saw a further 61 pupils go through the air gunnery training at Morpeth. Three were withdrawn as "sick" whilst a further two failed the course. The accuracy levels in terms of air-to-air firing was put at 30%, which may seem low but was actually 5% higher than No.24 Course's figure.

On 21st April 1943, the RAF's Bomb Disposal Organisation was re-organised into the form of squadrons, each containing four or more Flights, which were sometimes spread out over several counties. No.6207 (Bomb Disposal) Flight was formed at RAF Morpeth and came under the command of No.5131 (Bomb Disposal) Squadron, which also looked after Flights based in North Yorkshire. As well as defusing unexploded bombs dropped by the *Luftwaffe*, the unit was called on to assist in the recovery of crashed aircraft in the region that were known to have been carrying bombs. It is very likely that No.6207 (Bomb Disposal) Flight was posted to Europe along with the vast majority of the Bomb Disposal Units, in order to make safe the huge numbers of stockpiled enemy bombs lying around airfields in Germany and Austria. The parent unit, No.5131 Squadron, finally disbanded in 1948.

No.26 Course passed out on 24th April 1943. Another 60 cadets had arrived at Morpeth on 7th March, of which two were removed from the course due to failing exams and another pair withdrawn because of sickness. Out of No.24, No.25 and No.26 Courses, just one airman was recommended for a commission, and none were retained as instructors.

April 1943 set a record in that no aircraft accidents occurred, not even minor ones, even though some 1,133 flying hours were carried out in total. This figure had not been reached for some considerable time. However, the conditions during the month were not good for flying, with wind and gales hampering training. Despite the station having three runways, the wind direction at times meant that flying had to cease for the day.

The month also saw no fewer than a dozen new pilots being posted to No.4 Air Gunners School. This presented the instructional flying side of operations with a somewhat heavy burden. Apart from the aircraft earmarked for gunnery training and tow duties (the Bothas and Martinets), the station only had a single Miles Master Mk.II advanced trainer for piloting and tow line instruction. It appears that up until that point, many new pilots posted in simply had to "learn on the job" after a minimum of training themselves.

Clearly a new set of procedures was required, and these were drawn up and listed in the official records:

"An examination for the new Pilots on arrival on Flying Aids Regulations etc., was instituted. An 'inner' or bad weather circus tow line was tried out and found to be uneconomical in every respect and wasteful of time. However, a modified circus scheme was evolved under which a return trip along the tow line is made five miles out to sea, thus enabling firing to continue; preparations for the institution of this scheme began at the end of the month."

Upon arrival at Morpeth, all new pilots now had to attend a two-week Air Gunnery Course at the School before they were allowed to join their assigned Flight. By the end of April 1943, three pilots had gone through this new procedure. All claimed to have received a greater understanding and appreciation of the air-to-air firing exercises and therefore were in a much better position to fly their aircraft in ways that could only benefit the cadets. This of course was a vast improvement on the way that some of the original group of pilots had treated their duties, believing themselves to be little more than glorified bus drivers, and a waste of their flying skills.

Whilst the gun turrets used by the ground training elements of the course, plus those fitted to the Botha fleet had once been the same or similar to ones installed in front-line bombers, the same could not be said in the spring of 1943. The gap between what the cadets had to play with and what they would use once they reached front-line units was widening fast. This also hampered instructors, whose lack of knowledge of up-to-date equipment began to show. Once successful trainees ended up on training crews flying in much more modern aircraft, they sometimes had to spend time trying to understand the differences between what they had learned on and what they ended up using night after night. Therefore, a decision was made to temporarily attach instructors from No.4 Air Gunners School to No.10 School of Technical Training at Kirkham, situated near Blackpool, where they would receive one week's refresher training on more modern turrets.

A synthetic training device in the shape of a Free Gunnery Trainer arrived at Morpeth from Jurby on the Isle of Man in April 1943. This large piece of equipment needed its own shed or hangar building, and it was some time before one could be erected at RAF Morpeth. The Free Gunnery Trainer used a hydraulically-operated Fraser-Nash Type 16 gun turret, installed halfway up a scaffolding tower. Above this on a top platform, was a cam-operated projector. In addition, a floodlight mounted on gimbals illuminated a large circular screen in front of the scaffold tower, a diffuser merging this light with the general screen illumination. A vignette, comprised of a metal plate fixed to a rod, was placed in front of the floodlit area. A second vignette, a plate with a rectangular aperture cut into it, was placed in front of the projector, thus allowing the projected film to fill the aperture with an image of a darkened aircraft against a light background. The Fraser-Nash turret was fitted with a graticule projector so that the point being aimed at would show up on the screen. The trainee gunner looked through the hood of a standard Mk.IIIA free gun reflector sight, which was fitted with a yellow filter to mask the yellow future position spot (hidden from the trainee but not the instructor, which helped the latter judge the accuracy). To add to the realism, sounds of engine noise and gun fire were added. Fims had already been recorded depicting images of real Messerschmitt Bf 109s, Bf 110s and Heinkel He 111s making dummy attacks, captured examples of these aircraft being operated by the RAF's No.1426 (Enemy Aircraft Circus) Flight, which was colloquially known as "the RAFwaffe". Occasionally, the Trainer employed a Boulton Paul C Mk.IIA gun turret instead.

When the gun triggers were pulled by the trainee, this was noted by the instructor who pushed a button on a hit recorder. A pointer also moved around a dial, recording the number of hits until the assumed supply of ammunition had been expended. It was noted that many cadets chose to practice manipulation of the turrets in their spare time during the evening so they could gain experience.

Whilst the Shadowgraph and Free Gunnery Trainers were useful pieces of equipment, a more locally designed piece of kit proved less so, at least initially. The Morpeth Station Armoury designed and constructed an illuminated night target for the 200 yard Moving Target ground range. However, the metal used in its construction was not thick enough and 0.303-inch bullets simply cut straight through the target. Modifications were therefore required, and a supply of armour plating was "scrounged" from Messrs. Vickers-Armstrong Ltd. in Newcastle. The official log was quick to praise the inventiveness of the armoury section:

"The target is now very successful – a Morpeth invention for a change in the Group."

The illuminated night target was not the only invention to come from the station's staff in early 1943. A device for checking both the length and weight of Browning machine gun return springs was invented and put into service, as was a special jig for removing flash eliminators from the same weapons.

Whilst ways to improve the efficiency of training at Morpeth were always at the forefront of planning among senior officers, the station's anti-aircraft defences were not neglected. Several "Motley Stalk" gun mountings were installed during April 1943. These were cast concrete rings which offered a level of protection against blast and machine gun bullets to the gun crew. Twin Browning machine guns were fitted to a fixed mounting inside the ring. At least one of these emplacements can still be seen today, near to the remaining hangar building. It currently has a small tree growing through it.

April's flying hours totals were 635 for Bothas, 508 for Martinets and just six on the Master Mk.II. The Moth Minor "hack" only flew for an hour during the month. 232,400 rounds of 0.303-inch ammo were fired in air-to-air practice, plus another 179,800 during ground exercises.

Wing Commander Sandow paid Morpeth a visit on 5th May 1943. He was interested in finding out how many airmen had been sent to convalescent homes since the station opened in early 1942. Five had been sent to Callaly Castle and a further six to Ford Castle, both located in Northumberland, whilst another individual was taken to Nun Monckton outside York.

The inaugural meeting of Wings For Victory Week for Ashington had already been held in the town on 30th April, with Group Captain Louden addressing an interested group of attendees. A week later, on 7th May, he also gave a talk to the inaugural Victory Week For Morpeth meeting held at the Town Hall. That same night, the RAF Station Dance Band played at a dance held at Pegswood. The village was included in the Morpeth Rural District. The following day, Morpeth and Morpeth Rural District Wings For Victory Week fundraising began, with a target of £140,000 being set for the whole area. Several pieces of equipment were provided by the station for a "Type B" (i.e. unclassified) exhibition held at Morpeth Town Hall, beginning on the 8th. The following day, personnel from the station attended a parade at Linton village, north of Ashington, which also included members of the Home Guard and Civil Defence Services. A march past was performed for Group Captain Louden, the most senior officer present. On the 10th, Squadron Leader Dunkley and Flight Lieutenant Smith represented RAF Morpeth at a dance held at Stobswood, near Widdrington in Northumberland. This area also came under the purview of the Morpeth Rural District in terms of fundraising for Victory Week.

Having arrived at Morpeth on 27th March, No.27 Course passed out on 8th May 1943. It was the first course to incorporate air-to-ground firing practice into the syllabus. A record 64 cadets started gunnery training but only 56 passed the final exams. Five pupils were transferred for medical reasons, two left following requests to do so and another was withdrawn from the course due to sickness. Given that the course was running in the lighter late spring evenings at Morpeth, night training had to be carried out on occasions by use of dark goggles in daylight hours. On average, each pupil received just over four hours of this type of training in air-to-air firing drill, together with a further nine hours daylight practice.

On 10th May 1943, one of the School's Botha aircraft crashed at Hazeltonrigg, north of Rothbury, during a freak snowstorm. L6531 took off from Morpeth at around 0840 hours in company with another two Bothas and headed north. Just to the east of Alwinton, the three aircraft encountered the snowstorm and low cloud. Two of the training machines managed to find their way to the airfield at Boulmer and landed safely, but L6531, flown by a Polish pilot, Sergeant Stefan Zawilinski, crashed onto Hazeltonrigg Hill, killing him and the three trainee gunners onboard the aircraft. Leading Aircraftsmen Kenneth Bradley, Donald Campbell, and Harold Carter were all members of the RAF Volunteer Reserve and had joined No.29 Course at No.4 Air Gunners School just a month earlier. It is unclear why no instructor or navigator/wireless operator was onboard the aircraft when it took off from Morpeth. Without an instructor to assess their performance, how could the trainees have known whether they were shooting correctly or not?

At Hazeltonrigg Farm, further down the hill from the crash site, shepherd Alec Bland heard the impact caused by the Botha. Alerted by the local air-raid post that an aircraft had possibly crashed, and aided by his assistant, Jock Wilson, he set off up the hill to find the site of the possible crash. Due to the poor visibility that morning, both men had to abandon their search at around lunchtime, having failed to stumble across the aircraft. However, by early afternoon the mist cleared sufficiently enough for Bland and Wilson to see the aircraft lying on Hazeltonrigg Hill. They made their way up to the site and discovered the remains of the airmen in the smashed wreckage of the aircraft. Seeing there was nothing they could for the unfortunate aircrew, Bland and Wilson headed for the nearest house with a telephone and notified the local police.

Word soon reached RAF Morpeth, who immediately sent a party out to Hazeltonrigg. The officer in charge asked if Alec Bland would take them up to the site, and also requested he bring a horse and trailer so that the bodies could be removed. At some stage afterwards, another group this time from No.83 Maintenance Unit at RAF Woolsington (now Newcastle International Airport) arrived to take away what pieces of the wreckage could be salvaged. It was suggested by the inquiry into the crash that Sergeant Zawilinski had descended to find the bottom of the cloud layer, in an attempt to locate his exact position. Unfortunately, as in numerous other similar cases during the war, the cloud covered the tops of the nearby hills. The pilot was believed to have been trying to return to

Morpeth instead of diverting to the aerodrome at Boulmer, up the Northumberland coast, as his colleagues had done. Zawilinski was buried at St. Mary's Churchyard in Morpeth four days later.

A photo of Sergeant Stefan Zawilinski, the No.4 Air Gunners School pilot who was killed when his Botha aircraft crashed into Hazeltonrigg Hill in Northumberland in May 1943. (Unknown)

The Botha which crashed on Hazeltonrigg Hill had been with No.4 Air Gunners School for less than a month. Built at Blackburn's Dumbarton factory in 1941, it had served with a Bombing & Gunnery School at Millom in Cumbria and No.8 Air Gunners School at Evanton, north of Inverness. After an overhaul in March 1943,

L6531 was delivered to Morpeth from No.22 Maintenance Unit at RAF Silloth, on the west coast of Cumbria, on 17th April 1942.

A station-wide anti-gas exercise was conducted at RAF Morpeth on 17th April 1943. Even though there was no evidence that the enemy was about to use such weapons, precautions were deemed necessary in case of sudden gas attacks, especially if the Germans were to suddenly suffer from a series of irreversible and damaging defeats. The exercise at Morpeth was also attended by a large number of civilian Air Raid Precaution Organisation representatives, who were there to observe how such procedures were carried out on a large scale. A report detailing the events that took place can be found in the official No.4 Air Gunners School records. The summary reads as follows:

"The intention of this exercise was to familiarise personnel with the procedure to be adopted in conditions of chemical warfare, and to give trained reconnaissance and decontamination squads practical experience of their duties."

At 1400 hours that day, it was assumed for the purposes of the exercise that a chemical warfare attack had been conducted against RAF Morpeth. All ranks, regardless of position, donned their No.5 Anti-Gas clothing. In relays of 200 at a time, personnel were marched to a central point located on the airfield's Technical Site. There they were lectured and then given a demonstration by the Station's Gas Officer on the detection of gas, how to correctly don and wear anti-gas clothing and carry out personal decontamination. Following the lecture, personnel were dismissed and told to return to their normal duties. However, this was not the end of the story:

"At 1630 hours, the 'Gas Attack' alarm was sounded. All ranks paraded, correctly dressed, on the demonstration site where a Mustard Gas Mine was detonated. The reconnaissance party detected contamination on a building, the roadway, an MT [Motor Transport] vehicle and a defence post. The contaminated areas

were marked out and the decontamination squads set to work on the affected areas using bleach powder and a high pressure jenny."

Half-an-hour later, this decontamination work was completed and the "all clear" gas signal was given. A running commentary on the clean-up was given using the loudspeaker fitted to a police car from the Morpeth force. The assembled personnel were marched off to their duty stations, but not before concentrations of Adamsite (DM, or diphenylaminechlorarsine, a non-lethal, riot control gas that induced vomiting) and also Capsaicin (CAP, or 8-methyl-*N*-vanillyl-6-nonenamide, a similar gas) were unexpectedly thrown in among their ranks. The personnel duly donned their protective equipment as per the procedures they had just learned and practiced. The exercise ended at 1800 hours. Group Captain Louden reflected on the success of the exercise in his closing comments:

"The use of live Mustard Gas stimulated the interest of all personnel. There were approximately 1,000 airmen and airwomen at the demonstration and were so arranged that all had a good view of the contaminations and of the decontamination methods. It is considered that personnel derived a great deal of Benefit from the practical demonstration. The reconnaissance and decontamination squads had approximately 20 hours instruction and carried out their duties efficiently."

20th April saw a record daily total of 109 hours 35 minutes flying hours being reached. Most of No.4 Air Gunners School's aircraft would have needed to be available on the day to achieve that level of intensive operations, which was a credit to the maintenance staff at the station.

Two days later, No.28 Course passed out. Cadets from this intake were transported to the North Seaton gunnery range to train with the "Morpeth Night Illuminated Target". The nights were becoming shorter due to the approach of summer, and so fewer hours of darkness existed. Although the new invention was still successful, it was deemed necessary to be able to control the brilliance of any prevailing light, as some of the gunners struggled with its intensity.

Another station record was broken on 27th April, when 48,400 rounds of 0.303-inch ammunition were fired. Another new piece of equipment also turned up during the month when a Lloyd James Speech Recorder and Playback device arrived. It had been obtained from the General Post Office and was used for intercommunication and speech training practice. Trials using the recorder were carried out in May and June 1943.

In May 1943, a new long-distance towline known as the "distance circus" was tested, this proving to be a great success. It enabled the number of gunnery aircraft per sortie to be increased from three to four, saving time during each course. The overall number of flying hours actually increased, despite periods of bad weather over the airfield and the coastal ranges.

No.29 Course passed out on 29th May 1943, with 64 cadets being assigned to Morpeth on 17th April. Three were killed in the crash at Hazeltonrigg and another two were withdrawn due to sickness. Each pupil received around 11 hours daylight gunnery practice on the ground and a further three wearing night goggles on the illuminated night range. The average flying hours per cadet was 12 hours 40 minutes, which of course included the time it took to fly from the aerodrome to the offshore ranges and back during each of the air firing practice sessions.

During July of the same year, Spitfires serving with No.57 OTU's Advanced Course across at Eshott's satellite airfield, Boulmer, were involved in fighter co-operation duties with the gunnery aircraft at Morpeth. Aircraft from Acklington also took part during in these exercises during the same month. Two further transient units operated from the airfield during the spring and early summer of 1943. No.1614 (Anti-Aircraft Co-operation) Flight moved in from Cark in April with their Hawker Henley target tugs. Several de Havilland Tiger Moth aircraft were also apparently operated by the unit during its stay at Morpeth. The unit is believed to have worked with No.15 Light Anti-Aircraft Practice Camp, which was based at Whitby. The Henleys departed in June but were replaced by the

Taylorcraft Auster Mk.IIIs of "A" Flight, No.652 Squadron, which arrived at RAF Morpeth for a few weeks to help direct practice artillery shoots on the Otterburn Ranges. The latter unit arrived from Almondbank on 1st June 1943 and began work with the Army's 15th Division. "Shoots" were carried out at the Otterburn Ranges on the 14th and the Austers detached to Morpeth helped to "call in the shots". The aircraft carried artillery "spotters" equipped with radio, who would communicate the fall of shot to the gunners, to allow them to fire more accurately.

Also on 1st June 1943, 350 children and 400 adults, mainly young women, were addressed by Squadron Leader Cradock at Cambois School. So began the station's efforts in support of the local Wings For Victory Week fundraising efforts. Cradock, who was on the staff at RAF Morpeth, gave a talk to pupils and parents at Bedlington Grammar School the following day. "Bedlington Week" had a target of £60,000 and when the subscriptions had been counted up, some £89,207 had been pledged.

Trade training of WAAFs who previously operated barrage balloons elsewhere in the country started at Morpeth in June 1943, the personnel involved being re-trained as flight mechanics. The training started on 2nd June and used an Avro Manchester for this purpose. The gunnery school had somehow acquired Manchester Mk.I L7419/3748M, one of the early versions fitted with a third tail fin, as a ground instructional airframe. The type was an unreliable precursor to the much more famous Lancaster. It looked very much like its successor, but with only two engines. The code letters were painted over but were still legible: "UG-B2". On the starboard side of the aircraft's nose, just behind the front turret was a painting of "Dopey", of Snow White and the Seven Dwarves fame.

This aircraft had served with No.207, No.50 and No.408 Squadrons, being used in intensive trials whilst with the former. It was flown on at least 14 operations and involved in three separate accidents, all of which required repairs. The bomber ended its flying career with No.1654 Heavy Conversion Unit at Wigsley in Nottinghamshire, training pilots how to operate heavy bombers after training on smaller aircraft such as the Airspeed Oxford.

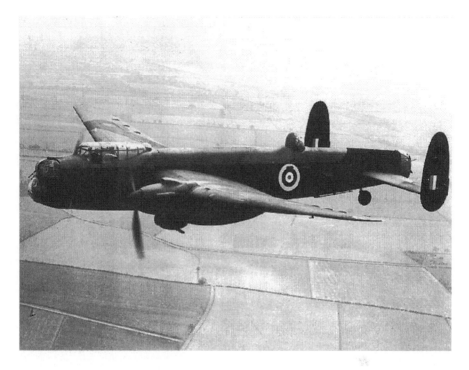

The Avro Manchester was designed to meet an Air Ministry specification for a twin engined bomber to replace the Whitleys, Hampdens and Wellingtons in service at the beginning of World War Two. The Rolls-Royce Vulture engines fitted to the type were unreliable and the entire fleet of Manchesters had to be grounded in April 1941 due to an ever increasing number of crashes. Avro re-designed the aircraft, adding two engines and replacing the Vultures with Merlins. This led to the extremely successful Lancaster bomber. Surviving Manchester aircraft were used as training machines or, like the example that arrived at Morpeth, ground instruction airframes. (Crown Copyright expired)

The Manchester was delivered to Morpeth by a crew from No.1654 Heavy Conversion Unit in early June 1943 and was then "parked" next to Flying Control during its time at the station. A very useful training tool, the machine was also used to give trainees experience of bomber aircraft fitted with turrets, but it soon had its outer wing sections removed. One story doing the rounds at the time was that the reason the Manchester had its wings "clipped" was that some of the Polish airmen stationed at the aerodrome wanted to use her on an unauthorised bombing raid on Germany! When word of this audacious plan reached senior officers, they instructed the station engineering staff to remove the outer wing sections so that it could no longer be made capable of flying! One hopes this story is true.

Weather was to blame for the loss of a Vickers Wellington Mk.1C twin-engined bomber that crashed just a couple of miles from the aerodrome on 2nd June. The aircraft, R1707/U, which belonged to No.20 Operational Training Unit at RAF Lossiemouth in Scotland, was on a navigational training exercise at night when its pilot, Flying Officer Allen Rossignol, encountered an electrical storm. He decided to divert to the nearest aerodrome, which was Morpeth. It is believed that the Wellington was struck by lightning as Rossignol was preparing to land and it crashed at Benridge Moor, near Pigdon. A local man, Joseph Wilkinson, witnessed the bomber on fire as it flew from west to east at low level, before ploughing through a hedge into a field where it exploded. It was also reported that the airframe had broken up prior to impact. Wreckage was strewn over a wide area. and all six crewmen onboard were killed. Allen Rossignol was an American serving with the RAF. Hailing from Washington D. C., he is buried in St. Mary's Churchyard in Morpeth. Also killed in the crash were Pilot Officer Adlard, Pilot Officer Fallon, Sergeant Morgan, Sergeant Faulkner and Sergeant Clarke.

No.20 Operational Training Unit was a training unit for recently-trained bomber pilots, navigators, bomb-aimers, wireless operators and gunners to gain experience in flying together as a newly-formed crew before they were posted to an operational squadron. Most of the trainees that passed the course at Morpeth would go onto one of these bomber Operational Training Units.

During their existence at Morpeth, around half of the School's Bothas were unfit for flight at any one stage, Mechanical failure occurred for a variety of reasons, but the Bristol Perseus Mk.X engines were known to be particularly susceptible to dust ingestion. At least 73 different Bothas served at Morpeth, the large numbers being necessary to allow for unserviceable machines. Clearly, this state of affairs could not be allowed to continue, since trained gunners were always in demand by Bomber Command. However, the unit had to wait for sufficient numbers of a replacement type to become available. Having two distinct makes of aircraft fulfilling the same role at the same aerodrome was not the most efficient way to run a training unit. Two separate amounts of spares would need to be kept on hand, for instance, and some pilots would have needed to go on refresher or conversion courses in order to fly another type of aircraft, even if they were performing the same sort of training flights.

An extremely important visitor on 4th June 1943 was General Sir Alan Brooke, Chief of the Imperial General Staff. It is not known when or how he arrived at RAF Morpeth, but he departed by air that day bound for an undisclosed destination.

No.30 Course passed out on 5th June 1943, and the trainees set a new record for No.4 Air Gunners School. All 60 of the group that began their training course passed, with no withdrawals or failures being recorded. This was in spite of bad weather cancelling all attempts to conduct air-to-ground firing practice and modifications to the night illuminated target denying them the use of that device. Each pupil had an average of 10 flying hours, with a similar number spent in the ground-based gun turrets.

A planned exhibition which was to be held at the aerodrome in support of Castle Ward's Wings For Victory Week on the 6th had to be postponed for three days due to bad weather. It went ahead on the 9th, visitors seeing the exhibits between 1800 and 2100 hours so as not to interfere with the intensive training operations.

The next major incident involving Bothas at Morpeth occurred at the nearby St. Mary's Hospital. Patients from Gateshead Mental Hospital had been transferred there on the outbreak of war to save them from the effects of bombing raids on Tyneside. L6441 suffered a failure of its starboard engine while on the final approach to the aerodrome on 9th June 1943. The pilot was believed to have "turned into the dead engine", which meant he had turned to the right after the starboard engine failed. This was not the correct procedure when something like this happened. Suspected "bearing failure" was given as the cause of the engine malfunction. The pilot, 22-year-old Pilot Officer Maciej Zaleski-Slubicz, another Polish airman, was killed when his aircraft exploded on impact in the grounds of the hospital. Also killed in the incident were the instructor, Sergeant N. A. Isherwood, and three trainee gunners, Leading Aircraftsmen Drummond, Ellis and Fane. Another trainee, Leading Aircraftsman Mason, survived the crash and was initially taken to the Station Sick Quarters before being transferred to the Royal Victoria Infirmary in Newcastle for treatment. Mason had suffered a fracture of his right lower third femur. Pilot Officer Zaleski-Slubicz was buried in the cemetery of St Mary The Virgin Church at Stamfordham on 12th June. His mother, Anna Puzynow-Zaleski, who died in 1986 aged 94, is also buried in the same plot and her name is listed on her son's gravestone. She had regularly sent money for the upkeep of her son's grave in Northumberland.

Apart from human error and mechanical failure, the Blackburn Botha also had a few tricks to play on unsuspecting pilots. In addition to its underpowered Bristol Perseus engines, one particular batch of aircraft suffered problems with their fuel control systems. If full power was held for too long during take-off and in the climb away from the aerodrome, then the aircraft's engines would suddenly cut. If one engine cut during take-off and the Botha was carrying full petrol tanks, then the pilot had to jettison some of the fuel in order to stay in the air. During dives, the aircraft's controls became rather heavy and were difficult to manage; a great deal of force was necessary to recover. A steep climb, therefore, was the usual result of such a recovery, which meant that the pilot once more had to apply force to return his machine to level flight. Even on the ground, the Botha posed problems. Taxying was occasionally a challenge as the aircraft was in danger of veering from side to side if the throttles were not handled gently enough. Civilian ferry pilots belonging to the Air Transport Auxiliary on the whole hated to fly the Botha as a result of its handling characteristics, but at least they were not delivering them all of the time. The servicemen of No.4 Air Gunners School did not have a choice in what their unit operated. The obsolete Bothas were available, still had flying hours to use up on the airframes, and so it was a case of taking what one was given.

Pilot Officer Ryszard Reszko, who was killed whilst trying to land at RAF Morpeth on 22nd June 1943, is buried in St. Mary's Churchyard in the nearby town. (Author)

However, by the beginning of 1943, it had been hoped that the Bothas would be phased out as soon as possible. Unfortunately, this did not occur until July of that year when the type was abruptly grounded at Morpeth, although some of the aircraft used by the School would lie abandoned on the aerodrome for several months afterwards. The replacement type of aircraft selected was the Avro

Anson; this was another aircraft that had been built for service with Coastal Command but was now relegated to second-line training duties. The new machines offered pilots a much better view of their trainee gunners in action, and the Armstrong Siddeley Cheetah engines fitted to the Ansons were much more reliable than the Bristol Perseus powerplants in the Bothas. The first two Ansons fitted with gun turrets turned up at Morpeth on 13th June 1943. The writing was clearly on the wall for the Botha.

RAF Morpeth's own Wings For Victory Week began on 19th June, with a fundraising target of £5,000 being set. The following day, the first of the year's Air Training Corps annual summer camps began, with four officers, two Warrant Officers and 63 other ranks turning up at the station.

No.31 Course passed out on 19th June. On the same day, the focus of Wings For Victory Week shifted across to Bellingham, in the North Tyne Valley. The village's target was set at £40,000. A parade held there was attended by two officers, 15 airmen and 15 WAAFs. The march past was taken by Group Captain Louden, who followed this up with a public address. A small number of pieces of equipment from the station were put on display for the assembled crowd.

The station may have been a forgotten backwater of the war, but it was still a busy one. Two of the "new" Ansons were actually cast-off from other units. These were Mk.Is N9977 and W2632/I, neither of which had gun turrets fitted. As they could not be used in gunnery practice flights, the two aircraft must have been acquired to allow the pilots at Morpeth to convert onto the new type. Each new type had its own foibles and so it was not simply a case of sitting in the seat, starting up the engines and taking off. Pilots had to undergo a quick conversion course, usually with a second pilot who was more conversant with the new type. The Ansons used by the trainee gunners were fitted with Bristol gun turrets which were designed to house two machine guns. However, at RAF Morpeth it seems as though only one gun was fitted in each turret. This was possibly due to shortages, as the front-line squadrons would have received priority over all supplies of weapons.

Another incident saw No.4 Air Gunners School suffering further casualties on 22nd June 1943 when Botha W5156 crashed on landing at Morpeth. On his final approach to the aerodrome, the pilot, Pilot Officer Ryszard Reszko, saw a red flare, which had been fired by the duty officer at Flying Control. The flare's meaning was obvious to all pilots: *"Do not land: go around again"*. As he climbed away, the Botha's two Perseus engines suddenly cut out, and the aircraft crashed. Pilot Officer Reszko, along with two of the trainee gunners onboard, Leading Aircraftsmen Frederick King and Harold Logan, were all killed in the incident. Reszko and Logan's graves can be found in St. Mary's Churchyard in Morpeth.

4th June 1943 saw a very successful Station Sports Day being held at the sports ground at the nearby Gateshead Mental Hospital. The event began at 1400 hours and ended seven hours later. Tea was provided for all participating personnel and prizes in the form of savings certificates and stamps were presented to the winners by Group Captain Louden's wife at a Station Dance later that evening in the Cadet's Dining Hall.

RAF Morpeth's Wings For Victory Week ended on the 26th, with £5,515-15'-6d being subscribed, over £500 above the target that had been originally set. The funeral of Pilot Officer Reszko had been held earlier the same day at St. Mary's Churchyard in Morpeth. The second Summer Camp of the year began on the 27th when two officers, two Warrant Officers and 71 other ranks from the Air Training Corps turned up at Morpeth from a local unit.

ANSONS, DRAUGHTY BILLETS & AIR EXPERIENCE FLIGHTS: JULY-SEPTEMBER 1943

One of the surviving Avro Anson Mk.Is is photographed flying in New Zealand in 2015. The type was used by the RAF in a huge number of different roles, from reconnaissance, anti-submarine patrol, electronic counter-measures, navigator training, wireless operator training, liaison, conversion course flying and light transport. No.4 Air Gunners School used its Ansons as gunnery trainers because the type was fitted with a single gun turret. These aircraft began replacing Bothas in 1943. (Oren Rozen, under Creative Commons licence)

By early July, No.4 Air Gunners School had not one but two Miles Master Mk.II training aircraft on strength; one was DK957/A, which had previously seen service with the RAF College and may have also been used as a "hack" (general duties) machine at Morpeth. The other example was DK957/B. Both of these were noted by Eric

Taylor on a visit in July 1943. The Masters were primarily used for "dummy attacks" on the Botha and Anson aircraft. This allowed the trainee gunners to have something "live" to aim at but not shoot at. DK957 later went onto become a station "hack" at Andrews Field and several other aerodromes. As there were no dual control Martinet tug aircraft, new pilots were checked out on the two Miles Masters. These two training aircraft were also used to show new pilots the towing areas off the coast.

The international flavour of the unit was demonstrated by some of the nationalities that had passed through the station before being posted to Operational Training Units. Apart from the Poles who flew the aircraft, there were Australian, Canadian, Dutch, Free French, New Zealanders and Norwegian trainee gunners at Morpeth. They would all be required to take the fight to Germany's cities and heavy industry.

Among the postings into RAF Morpeth during July 1943 was Acting Squadron Leader H. G. Plumridge, who took up the post of Chief Technical Officer on the 14th. He had previously served down at RAF Cranwell in Bedfordshire. Dorothy Loltgen was a WAAF who arrived at RAF Morpeth to take up the trade of instrument maker in July 1943. Her experience there was probably typical of most WAAFs that were posted to the station. She arrived at Morpeth railway station in the middle of the night:

"The R. T. [radio telegraphy] Office was closed, and the only person around was the Station Master, who got through to one of the Transport Officers in one of the camps. They sent a van to take us to the camp. We arrived at the cook house, the staff were cross at having to provide us with food. They gave us baked beans without any bread, and because we had left our kit bags in the van we had to eat with our fingers."

Dorothy's life at Morpeth did not get any easier, and her recollections are a reminder of just have primitive life on an RAF station, especially a "temporary" one built during the mid-war period could be:

"Our billets were in a field just outside the camp, we found out that the three huts we were living in had just been condemned by the Medical Officer. These places were very isolated, there was one stove and three lots of cupboards down the middle, this is where we hung our great coats, which were only worn in the winter."

When one of her colleagues came to put her coat on one morning, she found mice nesting in the pockets. Even the local farm animals appeared to resent the presence of the WAAFs:

"The wash house looked out over the fields where there were cattle, but there was no glass in the window. We put up a line from the window to the fence to hang our smalls on. One day I was told that the cows were eating my stockings and I was put on a charge for neglect of my uniform. I had to prove that I was telling the truth, so I had to bring witnesses along to tell them that I had not damaged them myself, and that I had retrieved them from the cow."

Dorothy Loltgen worked on some of the instruments fitted to the cockpits of the various aircraft types based at Morpeth:

"I worked on adjustments on the instruments. I had to use watchmakers tools which were very fine. We worked on the blind flying panel which is still in existence today on every aircraft today. On it was the air speed indicator and altimeter. The air speed indicator was worked from air pressure from a pitot head which was fixed at the end of the wings, air went through the pitot head and through to the instrument measuring air speed. This is the sort of instrument that I learnt the inside of and how to service it."

No.32 Course completed its training on 3rd July 1943. 60 pupils had started their training on 23rd May, and one had failed the final exams. Another was transferred onto No.34 Course for reasons unknown. The fates of two more cadets is unknown, as only 56 pupils passed out. Three of them were recommended for commissions. The firing exercises using night goggles were no' carried out due to adverse weather towards the end of the course. It was agreed that future courses would perform this training earlier on in the syllabus so that trainees could benefit from the practice.

Three officers and 55 other ranks of the Air Training Corps' Newcastle Wing arrived on the 4th for a week's detachment. The air cadets received lectures, were shown pieces of equipment and even had a flight in one of the School's Anson aircraft. Gateshead Wing turned up the following week and Tynemouth the week after that. The final summer camp of the month saw the Longbenton contingent arrive at Morpeth on the 25th. One of the cadets in the latter group was Eric Taylor. Although the station was only used for training and therefore did not receive the amount of visiting aircraft that an active base had, he still noted a couple of interesting visitors during his six days there. One of these was Fairchild Argus HM168, presumably on Air Transport Auxiliary duties, while the other was Spitfire Mk.VB AD288/MN-G from No.350 Squadron, a Belgian fighter squadron that was based at RAF Acklington during July 1943. Aircraft from the squadron had been escorting convoy "Kingsmith" northbound up the coast that morning. This aircraft ended its days in France after the war as a ground instruction airframe. Eric was supposed to have made his first flight in Avro Anson MG111, with a Polish pilot detailed to fly the twin-engined aircraft:

"The ground crews were unfamiliar with the Anson, which had only been in use for a few days, and couldn't get the engines started. The pilot, after much cursing, said 'Give me back my Botha" and walked away, so I didn't get my flight!"

Eric also recalled his first flight, which gives a good idea of what the gunners had to do during their training:

"I made my first ever flight in Anson LV298 on 30th July 1943 — not everyone's first flight is made in an aircraft that fires its guns! We took off, I wound up the undercart, the Martinet arrived (No.12) and the three gunners shot at the drogue, and we returned to base. The Martinet flew on a parallel course to the Anson, but at the end of

each run, the Martinet turned through 180 degrees and flew back the way it had come. As it turned more quickly than the drogue, there would come a point where the Martinet, drogue and Anson were all in line. The pilot then had to shout at the gunner to stop firing, or he might hit the Martinet. I also noticed that if the gunner's shots were going a little too high or low, a gentle bank by the pilot would put the shots back on target."

A later flight was a little more eventful:

"I had a second flight (...) which should have been in the Oxford (...) but ended up in Anson LV161. On this occasion, after the first gunner had started firing, the gun jammed and could not be cleared. There was some chatter between the pilot and crew, which I couldn't really understand, and the pilot made some hand signals to the Martinet pilot (no radio contact). The Martinet (HP480/9) came alongside and after some more hand signals, flew away. We returned to Morpeth and landed. I picked up my observer type parachute from the rear of the Anson and walked away. One of the gunners hurried after me and asked me not to tell anyone what had happened, which was easy, as I didn't know what had happened. He then told me that the gun had been in use for much of the day and was hot, causing the jamming. It seemed that, rather than admit they couldn't handle this, the gunners dumped the remaining ammunition in the sea — not an unusual occurrence, it seemed."

Senior staff visits continued apace during July 1943. On the 5th, Squadron Leader Pryer arrived from Flying Training Command Headquarters for the purpose of looking into possible arrangements for the local training of flight mechanics. Pryer was part of the Command's Engineering Staff and wanted to know if Morpeth could help train selected personnel to become engine fitters and the like. Suitably trained and proven mechanics, especially reliable ones, were rare commodities so any methods of increasing their numbers was worth looking at.

No.33 Course passed out on the 10th. In terms of the number of pupils who failed to make the grade, it was the worst that Morpeth had seen. 61 cadets began their training on 30th May and yet only 47 passed their final exams. One was disciplined for unknown reasons and dismissed from the course. Four more were withdrawn at their own request and another transferred to No.36 Course due to sickness. Two cadets failed their exams, and another ended up in hospital due to an air crash. This left five pupils whose reasons for not passing have not been recorded.

On 12th July, Pilot Officer Hayton from No.29 (Training) Group turned up at Morpeth to judge the Dining Hall in connection with the Group's Dining Hall Competition. When the results were finally known sometime later, Morpeth had been placed second in the entire Group, losing out only to RAF Evanton.

No.34 Course passed out on the 17th. The failure rate was much improved as only two pupils from the original 61 did not make it as far as the final exam. One was withdrawn as sick and the other was failed in a progressive examination. Once again, bad weather was to blame for hampering the flying training programme. This time it was the air-to-ground element of the syllabus that could not be carried out.

Shortly before the Bothas were removed from service with No.4 Air Gunners School, there was time for one more incident. Botha Mk.I W5044, flown by Sergeant Ball, force-landed on the aerodrome on the 17th due to engine failure. The aircraft struck Anson LV162, which happily was unoccupied at the time. Onboard the Botha were the instructor, Corporal Crafer, plus two trainees, Leading Aircraftsmen Cupe and Foster, and a member of the Air Training Corps, Corporal Bates. None were hurt in the incident.

The aforementioned plans to merge the medical staffs from RAF Morpeth and nearby Stannington finally came to fruition on 20th July 1943. Air Commodore Hewat, the Principal Medical Officer from Flying Training Command, visited the station in concert with Wing Commander Wilson, Senior Medical Officer from No.29 (Training) Group. The final obstacles to merging the medical staff were discussed in various meetings, and the changes were laid out in the official records:

"The Sick Quarters at Stannington was to be closed apart from a medical inspection room and Class A stores returned to Hartlebury [No.25 Maintenance Unit, located near Kidderminster, which was a huge storage facility for RAF equipment]. The rooms, however, were to be kept for emergency use if necessary. Officers and other ranks from Stannington were to be accommodated in Sick Quarters Morpeth. These changes were to be effected forthwith."

The universally unloved Bothas were suddenly withdrawn from use sometime between the 17th and the 25th of the month. By this time, enough Ansons had been delivered to maintain the scheduled gunnery training programme. However, the new machines were not without their own problems. Flying Officer J. Roberts had a lucky escape on 30th July whilst piloting Anson Mk.I LV299 over the Druridge Bay air-to-air firing ranges. Sudden engine failure meant that he had to look for a place to set the stricken aircraft down. With some skilful flying, he was able to force-land the Anson at RAF Acklington.

No.35 Course passed out on 31st July 1943. 62 cadets started their training on 20th June and 55 managed to pass the final exam. Of the seven who did not make the grade, one was withdrawn from the course due to being discovered to be under-age. Another pupil was disciplined and then dismissed. Three failed the final exam and another two were transferred onto later courses. The average number of flying hours was recorded as ten, with another two hours using night goggles due to the long evenings.

By the end of July 1943, No.4 Air Gunners School had trained its 2,000th pupil, quite an achievement for the unit. Group Captain Louden complimented the School's instructors on this feat, and on the enthusiasm and keenness they had showed since the unit had been formed. The Bothas had been completed replaced by Ansons and it had already been recognised that the instructor had a better view of his pupil in action when flying in the new type. All of the pilots on the Gunnery Flight had converted to the new aircraft during the month but their training had not affected the gunnery flight programme in any way. Officers had liaised with staff at Acklington and Boulmer to see whether fighter aircraft could be spared from their normal duties at these stations to provide effective targets for cine-gun camera exercises. Such training proved to be beneficial to both the School and the fighter pilots, especially in the case of the Boulmer personnel. It was home to the Advanced Flight from No.57 Operational Training Unit based across at Eshott, which trained airmen who were fresh out of basic flying to become fighter pilots. The Advanced Flight at Boulmer relieved some of the pressure at the busy airfield next to the Great North Road and simulated some elements of the missions that the shiny new pilots would undoubtedly face once they joined a front-line squadron. Having live targets in the shape of Ansons flying up and down the coast was much better than any synthetic training, and the dummy attacks the trainee pilots provided extremely useful experience for the gunnery pupils.

Cine cameras were also added to the gun turrets so that the results of firing practice could be recorded and played back to the trainees. This became an important part of the gunnery course at Morpeth. Dorothy Loltgen was also involved in servicing this equipment:

"I was sent on a refresher course to learn about the camera gun. A 16mm film was put into a cartridge instead of bullets, the casing which held the bullets was replaced by the casing which held the camera. I had to learn the electric circuit of the camera, which was used to train the air gunners how to shoot accurately. The aircraft trailed a drogue behind, and it flew ahead followed by the trainer aircraft with the camera gun. Afterwards we showed the film on a screen, it showed the markings and how accurate the air gunner's shooting was, and how they could improve it."

The urgent need for air gunners to replace losses and help form new squadrons can be demonstrated by looking at the log book of one particular trainee in July 1943. R. S. Routledge, part of No.35 Course, began his practice flying at Morpeth on 18th July 1943 and completed his airborne part of the syllabus on the 27th, having only amassed 12 hours 15 minutes worth of flying before being passed by Squadron Leader L. Atkinson, Officer Commanding, Training Wing, No. 4 Air Gunners School. These hours were relatively equally spread out over twelve separate training flights, one of which had to be scrubbed due to poor weather conditions. The newly-promoted Sergeant Routledge joined No.44 Squadron in March 1944, which operated Lancasters, and became part of Flight Sergeant Young's crew. After surviving an operational "tour", he became a gunnery instructor himself, serving with No.11 Air Gunners School at Andreas on the Isle of Man in February 1945.

Some Botha aircraft were flown out of Morpeth during July 1943 to be handed over to other units or put into temporary storage at various Maintenance Units pending a decision being made as to what to do with them. The remaining machines sat rather forlornly at various points around the aerodrome, with an uncertain future awaiting them.

Consett Air Training Corps Squadron's arrived at Morpeth on 1st August 1943, with three officers and 60 other ranks enjoying a week long attachment. A week later, it was the West Hartlepool unit's turn. The Gateshead Wing returned for a second week on the 15th, being accompanied by members of the Rowlands Gill detachment. The final week long camp of the month was hosted for the Newbiggin Air Training Corps Squadron, with two officers and 27 other ranks appearing on the 22nd. In addition to attending lectures and parades, the cadets were something of a godsend to personnel at the station as they were often tasked with general "fatigue" type duties – peeling potatoes, cleaning floors, etc. Even though weather conditions were not always suitable for flying during the month, every cadet that visited Morpeth was given at least one flight.

Group Captain Franklyn, Wing Commander Openshaw and five other officers arrived from No.29 (Training) Group Headquarters on 2nd August for an Air Staff Inspection. This was followed up over the next few weeks by visits from the Group's Physical Fitness

Officers and Flying Training Command's Catering Branch, the latter inspecting the mess arrangements at the station. There was also a visit by the Command's Salvage Branch, presumably to check on how RAF Morpeth dealt with broken equipment. Requisitions for new "kit" came at the expense of labour and materials that could be used more efficiently elsewhere, so cutting down on orders for new equipment was encouraged where possible. Judging by the number of official visits for one part of the aerodrome or another each month, it appeared that there was a never-ending stream of official inspections. Even so, the gunnery training at Morpeth continued without pause.

Squadron Leader T. A. Hudson, who had been Senior Medical Officer since April 1943, departed for Brize Norton in Oxfordshire on 6th August. A new arrival on the spiritual side of things was Reverend Squadron Leader F. Matthews, a Church of England Chaplain who was posted in from RAF Locking in North Somerset on the 10th. There was a fair amount of churn in terms of incoming and outgoing pilots during August 1943 with four arrivals and eight leaving the station.

No.36 Course passed out on the 14th. 62 started the course and there were four failures. Shotgun firing had been limited by a hold-up in the supply of clays to the station. In addition, synthetic parachute training had been cancelled due to the apparatus being declared unserviceable, although remedial action was carried out before the end of the following course. The air-to-ground targets used in training were being rebuilt to resemble tanks and other vehicles, which provided cadets with a "real world" situation.

The only flying accident during the month occurred on the 15th when Martinet JN430's brakes failed. The aircraft was being piloted by Sergeant J. B. Barker at the time and ran off the runway. Damage was minor and the machine was later repaired.

Air Commodore E. W. Norton, Air Officer Commanding No.29 Group, arrived for an inspection on 20th August. Eric Taylor visited Morpeth again that day with the Longbenton Air Training Corps Unit in order to gain some flight experience. A twin-engined

Airspeed Oxford, serial number AB685, had turned up in order to give same of the air cadets a ride, but its pilot had other ideas:

"The pilot declared his aircraft was unserviceable, so he had his lunch and flew away again!"

Having started its training on 11th July, No.37 Course completed its training on 21st August. 61 cadets were assigned to the intake. Two were withdrawn for medical reasons, two failed the final exams and one was transferred to No.39 Course. Bad weather at the end of the course resulted in both the air-to-air and air-to-sea averages being slightly below syllabus requirements. Sea targets were used due to the ground targets still being converted into objects that looked like tanks and trucks from the air. The synthetic parachute equipment was still unserviceable at the start of the course, but repairs ensured it could be used later on.

Another visit connected with the Air Training Corps occurred on the 22nd when Air Chief Marshall Sir Robert Brook-Popham arrived to inspect the cadet unit attached to Morpeth. On the same day, Air Marshall Sir Philip Babington, Air Officer Commanding in Chief, Flying Training Command, inspected the station. It is not known whether another flying demonstration was arranged for his benefit but if one was, it did not end in disaster as had occurred in March.

The last course to pass out during August was No.38, which did so on the 28th. 60 pupils started on 17th July and 54 made the grade, three failing their final exams and another three withdrawing from the course. Again, the average scores for air-to-air firing practice were slightly below syllabus requirements due to weather conditions, and work on the ground targets meant that float targets on the offshore ranges were used instead. Even though the scores had not achieved what was expected, the trainees still passed as allowances were clearly made due to mitigating factors.

August 1943 was regarded as a very successful month in terms of training at Morpeth. It was the first one in which Ansons were the sole gunnery aircraft employed. In total, 240 airmen were under instruction during the month, of which 168 passed out successfully.

One was commissioned and a further two retained as instructors. Nine failed their final exams and the others withdrew from courses at their own request or on medical grounds. To give some idea of the nationalities involved, the 240 included seven Dutch, seven Free French and eight Norwegian nationals. One of the Norwegians had to withdraw on medical grounds.

In addition, August saw a record number of flying hours notched up, with over 1,650 being recorded. Out of those, 1,528 were noted as "productive", the others being travel time to and from the ranges or training flights that were scrubbed due to bad weather or aircraft malfunction. This figure beat the old record by at least 200 hours.]

Also in August 1943, night flying was introduced at RAF Morpeth by order of the Air Officer Commanding. Initial flights were carried out to inspect the newly-installed airfield lighting equipment which was almost complete. Subsequent flights were, however, restricted to five miles from the airfield. Such missions were used to assess the potential of staff pilots carrying out other duties, including operations against the enemy. By that stage, No.4 Air Gunners School had twenty-three Avro Anson air gunnery trainers and twenty-five Miles Martinet target tugs on establishment, in addition to the remaining Bothas destined for the scrapyard. 11 of the latter were ferried from Mopeth during August 1943. Of the new Ansons, two had been fitted with dual controls but no gun turrets. These were N9977 and W2632, which were used to check out new pilots on so-called "circuits and bumps". They had also been used to convert existing pilots from the Bothas.

No.39 Course passed out on 11th September 1943. 61 pupils were joined by another transferred from No.37 Course. 57 passed out, four failed the exams and another was transferred to No.42 Course. One of the successful gunners was retained at Morpeth as an instructor.

On the 14th, Group Captain Louden attended a public meeting at Morpeth Town Hall where he presented the Mayor with a Wings For Victory plaque and a Certificate of Honour which had been conferred upon the town in recognition of its population achieving its savings target during the recent fundraising campaign.

Bricks from countless manufacturers were used in the construction of the buildings at RAF Morpeth. "Lily" was made by Priestman Collieries Limited, who took over the Lily Drift at Rowlands Gill in 1901 and supplied a number of local coal mines. "Lily" bricks were also used in the construction of the Newcastle Airport Hotel and the Nuffield Hospital in Jesmond, Newcastle. The brick in the photograph is part of a huge pile lying at the northern end of the old Runway 23. (Author)

The following day, there was a full station colour hoisting parade at RAF Morpeth, which was held to commemorate the anniversary of the Battle of Britain. Group Captain Louden took the parade and a special religious thanksgiving service was held afterwards.

23rd September saw a flying visit from one of the Ministry of Aircraft Production's "Action Squads". Led by Squadron Leader J. E. Avery, it conducted a thorough check to make sure that Morpeth had no equipment that was surplus to its requirements. Such "kit" should have been declared and transferred to other units which needed it. Of course, technical and engineering staff were always happy to have "spares" of various equipment on hand in case of malfunctions and breakages, so it is likely that some consumables, particularly smaller items of equipment that could be hidden away easily, escaped the "Action Squad's" beady eyes!

On 25th September 1943, a couple of Fairey Aircraft Company types, the Swordfish torpedo-spotter-reconnaissance biplane and the Barracuda torpedo bomber, gave flying demonstrations at RAF Morpeth for the benefit of employees from two local companies that were manufacturing parts for these aircraft. One of these was Northern Coachbuilders Limited and the other was the North East Aircraft Corporation, based in Gateshead. Altogether, 132 employees from the two companies attended the event. Both firms had taken on contracts to supply parts for various types. Employees from both companies were taken up to Morpeth to see a flying display by the "Stringbag" and the "Barra". Outings such as this one, organised by the Ministry of Aircraft Production, were considered to be a morale booster for the workforce and no doubt those employees lucky enough to attend were very pleased to see the fruits of their labour in the skies above Morpeth. However, it is not known which particular aircraft were involved, nor the units they belonged to. The average number of flying hours was recorded as 17 hours 40 minutes, which was arguably the highest yet.

On the same day, No.40 Course passed out with another 57 out of the original 61 managing to pass their final exams. However, one pupil was withdrawn from the course due to discipline problems and another for medical reasons. Whilst none were retained at RAF Morpeth as instructors, three were at least recommended for commissions so they must have impressed senior staff.

Also on the day the Fleet Air Arm turned up, 17 other ranks from six separate Air Training Corps squadrons arrived at Morpeth for a week-long detachment. These cadets were from Nos. 131, 346, 404, 1000, 1126 and 1156 Squadrons. It is not known why such a small number were involved.

On the 26th, contingents of RAF and WAAF personnel took part in parades held at Morpeth town centre in the morning and across at Bedlington in the afternoon. These events were further commemorations for the Battle of Britain. On both occasions, the salute was taken by Squadron Leader Cradock instead of Group Captain Louden, but there was a good reason for this. There was about to be a change of commander at the RAF station.

Overseeing the employees' day was one of the last official duties that Group Captain John Louden performed at Morpeth, as he departed the station on 27th September, being posted to No.29 (Training) Group Headquarters pending a transfer to an overseas station. John Louden had overseen a dramatic improvement in training procedures whilst in command at Morpeth, with increases in flying hours and numbers of successful cadets.

Morpeth now had a new commanding officer in the shape of, Group Captain Athol Fear. The fifth officer appointed to command the station, Fear had entered the RAF in 1932, flying Hawker Audax biplanes with No.26 Squadron at Catterick in North Yorkshire. Pilot Officer Fear was lucky to survive a crash in the Pentland Hills, just south of Edinburgh, whilst flying his Audax on 15th June 1934. After war was declared, he served as Officer Commanding, No.1 Air Gunners School, RAF Pembrey in South Wales. The unit operated Bristol Blenheim light bombers which had been retired from front-line duties and were more highly regarded than the Bothas had been at Morpeth. Group Captain Fear immediately swapped DH.94 Moth Minor X5133 (the impressed civilian aircraft G-AFPH) for Avro Tutor K3526 as his personal "runabout". This soon became the commanding officer's pride and joy, being based at Morpeth until 25th April 1944.

September's figures must have been good news for the recently appointed Group Captain Fear, as they showed a new record for the number of hours flown, 1,900 hours 30 minutes. This was at least 200 hours more than the previous record, which had only been set the month before. On the negative side, No.4 Air Gunners School lost nine pilots, seven of which went straight to front-line units. The other two were transferred to different training units within No.29 Group, probably to make up for shortages. However, these losses in the flying staff were soon rectified by the arrival of another nine pilots, six of which needed a rapid conversion course on the aircraft they were destined to fly whilst at the School. Three had turned up at the end of the month and their own conversion courses were yet to be completed. As for aircraft accidents, there were only two to report during September. Both occurred whilst the aircraft were on the ground. One happened because the pilot elected to retract his undercarriage before the aircraft had taken off, and the second occurred because of brake failure, the machine colliding with another on the taxiway. Neither involved injury although extensive repairs were needed in both cases.

BULLETS & BULLETINS: OCTOBER-DECEMBER 1943

This relic appears at first glance to be a Pickett-Hamilton retractable gun position, which was designed to be lowered into the ground when not in use, so as not to interfere with the movement of aircraft. Installed at many airfields across Britain during the early "invasion scare" period of 1940 to 1941, it was found that their roofs could not support the weight of new heavy bombers such as the Halifax and Lancaster. However, the lack of gun slits just below its roof (just below the hatchway) suggest that it may be the outer sleeve that the fort retracted into. (Author)

No.41 Course passed out on 2nd October 1943, being replaced by No.45 Course. 60 cadets had started this course on 22nd August, of which just 52 passed. Three failed the final exam, another three were withdrawn at their own request, one was withdrawn for unspecified medical reasons, whilst another became so airsick he could not continue. It was clearly impossible to weed out cadets such as the latter before they turned up to begin aircrew training.

No.42 Course passed out on the 9th and No.46 Course arrived at Morpeth the same day. 59 cadets had begun No.42 Course on 28th August, and once again just 52 passed the final board exam. Two failed these whilst a third was removed due to discipline. One of the two failures had managed a 68% score on guns but failed the course anyway. The other failed both the gun and sighting exams. Four more pupils were transferred to subsequent courses. However, one successful gunner was retained as an instructor.

No.4 Air Gunners School began issuing its own *"Weekly Training Bulletin"* in October 1943. Each edition was a single page long and provided details of the training syllabus, together with news, details of soon-to-be-arriving Courses and other items of related interest to instructors and staff. It was published each Thursday and its purpose was listed as follows:

"Its aim is to discuss methods of training at this Unit, so that the present high standard may be maintained and, if possible, improved. This Bulletin will contain notes and notices concerning the instructional staff generally and it is hoped that members of the staff will contribute suggestions etc., to be incorporated in the Bulletin. These should be sent to Flight Lieutenant Robson."

Issue No.1 mentioned Flight Lieutenant Gould, who had recently departed No.4 Air Gunners School, but not before producing a Gun and Turret Syllabi which were now available for instructors. It was imperative that the latter were all focussed on their work:

"These syllabi fulfil a long-felt need and it is hoped that instructors will make full and correct use of them. Although we are now fully organised in this respect, we must not lose sight of the fact that however comprehensive a syllabus may be, the pupils learn only by the skill of the instructor to impart his own knowledge. Let us therefore see if we can improve our lectures by -

a) Always showing enthusiasm for our subject.
b) Carefully preparing each lecture.
c) Making the lectures interesting and instructive."

A named officer, Flight Lieutenant Le Sueur, was quoted as being responsible for all aspects of the cine and instructional film side of training. It was hoped that instructors who had suggestions how to improve this, and dummy attacks by the Martinet tug aircraft, were to be passed onto him. It was also remarked that damage had been done to a fully working model of the Frazer Nash gun turret system, apparatus which had been the result of many months' worth of hard work. Instructors were therefore reminded to exercise case when using it. A further piece of instruction equipment in the shape of an Anson fuselage was mentioned. This was located in a hangar situated on the Instructional Site at RAF Morpeth and was used for ditching drill, although it was not quite ready for use by the start of October 1943. It was extremely important that trainee gunners learned how to prepare for an aircraft landing in the sea, especially as most of their airborne training was over water. It had therefore been decided that in addition to the land-based training using the Anson fuselage, trainees would practice taking up ditching stations in the aircraft as they returned from the ranges. This would not occur on every flight, but it was to happen frequently, so the cadets quickly learned the procedure.

In addition to giving details of the courses, the *Weekly Training Bulletin* became a useful vehicle in which to impart information about former trainees who had passed through the station. Whilst no actual names were given for obvious reasons, general details were provided. The following was included in *Bulletin No.2*:

"It has come to our knowledge that cadets from as recent a course as No.38 are already on operational squadrons and have done from 3 to 5 ops. On arrival at OTU [Operational Training Unit, where new crews were put together and had intensive practice in simulated bombing missions, conducted over Britain in realistic conditions], they were examined, and their standard was such that they were

immediately posted to Conversion Units, whilst gunners from other schools were retained for further training."

Further praise was heaped upon the instructors at Morpeth:

"There is evidence of the increasing goodwill of OTUs towards Morpeth trained Air Gunners and this is a tribute to our high standard of instruction. This happy state of affairs can only be kept up by maintaining the present system (which has been built up through 18 months of hard work) and by sustaining our characteristic spirit of co-operation between all concerned in the training of Air Gunners at 4 A. G. S."

23rd October saw No.43 Course passing out, and it was replaced at the station by No.47 Course. The success rate was falling: 62 started No.43 Course but only 50 passed. Four failed the final exam, five were withdrawn and three more transferred to other courses. The third *Weekly Training Bulletin* started with an analysis of why this particular course had fared so badly:

"An investigation into the reasons for the deplorable results on No.43 Course Progressive Examination has brought to light several interesting points, not the least of which is expressed in the following.

A Cadet on interrogation said that it was commonly supposed that the Air Gunners' training was a 'piece of cake'. His particular course had been told at a previous Unit that gunners were badly needed and that there was little chance of failure.

This belief, no doubt, contributed largely to a collective failure (51.85%) after three weeks' instruction. Needless to say, the people concerned have had a rude awakening."

It was made clear that everyone involved in the training of gunners was to take every opportunity to impress upon cadet the necessity for concentration and hard work throughout their course. There was recognition that other Gunners' Schools had possibly indulged in the dubious practice of "pushing through" cadets who had failed to reach the necessary standard, but that was not going to happen at Morpeth. There would be no special treatment for those who failed the final board exam.

One former No.4 Air Gunners School pupil was however named in *Weekly Training Bulletin No.3*, and news of his success during one particular raid must have cheered up the hard-working instructors at Morpeth after the poor results recorded on No.43 Course:

"Sgt. William Leary, of Rex Street, Hulme, Manchester, mid-upper gunner in a Lancaster bomber, shot up a F. W. 190 [Focke-Wulf Fw 190 fighter, occasionally used by night-fighter units over Germany] just before reaching Bochum in Wednesday night's big RAF raid and later over the target shot down a Ju. 88 [Junkers Ju 88, a twin-engined bomber type which was also used as a night-fighter] and scored hits on another enemy machine. In a raid over Germany on Thursday last he shot down a Ju. 88 and damaged two others. Sgt. Leary joined the RAF before he was 18 and has completed over 50 operational flights."

William Leary had been part of No.26 Course at Morpeth. He joined No.61 Squadron at Syerston in Lincolnshire and became the mid-upper (dorsal) turret gunner in Pilot Officer F. J. Nixon's crew. On the Bochum raid mentioned above, Leary was flying in JB138, of the unit's Lancaster bombers.

By the time *Bulletin No.3* had been issued, the Anson fuselage ditching drill training aid was ready for use. It was stressed upon instructors that cadets were not to be let anywhere near it or inside it when they were not present or engaged in other duties.

26th October saw an official visit by Air Commodore L. G. Croke, Air Officer Commanding, No.29 (Training) Group. After inspecting all areas of the station, he stayed overnight, attending a "Dining In" night which was held in the Officers Mess in his honour. It was stated in *Weekly Training Bulletin No.4* that Air Commodore Croke had been suitably impressed with the School. He was pleased by the syllabus's Initial Test, the model of the Fraser Nash gun turret system (which had been repaired and was in use again), plus the voice recording apparatus which had been introduced earlier that same year. The Initial Test was a new part of each course, and ran as follows:

"At 08.00 on the first day of the course, cadets are given a paper which contains 20 questions. There are ten intelligence aptitude questions supplied by the Station Education Officer, and ten technical questions which cover guns, turrets and aircraft recognition. Short answers only are required, and space is provided for them on the question paper.

The results of the test are used to:

1) Assess individual cadets on arrival.

2) Assess the course as a whole.

3) Grade the course, for squadding purposes."

The cadets of No.47 Course were selected as guinea pigs for the new test and the results were listed. No-one had scored 100% but 25 out of the initial 50 achieved 70% or higher. Instructors were asked to keep the scores confidential, presumably so as not to demoralise pupils or make others think they could slacken off.

On 28th October 1943, Group Captain Fear travelled across to Bellingham to attend a public meeting where he presented the Mayor with the town's "Wings For Victory" plaque and a Certificate of Honour. Bellingham had achieved its savings target during the Wings For Victory Week campaign earlier in the year.

Even though bad weather and shorter daylight hours were a feature of October, No.4 Air Gunners School managed to reach a total of 1,017 hours 35 minutes flying time, which was no mean feat. No flying accidents were reported during the month. Four pilots were posted out, but the deficit was soon made up by an equivalent number of arrivals, who required conversion courses. 49 staff pilots were recorded as being on the unit's strength at the end of the month.

Weekly Training Bulletin No.5 appears to have been the last one retained for posterity, or it may have just fizzled out, especially if the person responsible for it was posted away.

I found this brick cable cover at the side of the footpath through the trees on the northern edge of the old aerodrome. (Author)

13th November 1943 saw the passing out of No.44 Course. It was replaced by No.48 Course, the only one to arrive at Morpeth during that month. As for No.44, 64 cadets had begun the course and only four failed to pass. Two were suspended due to failures in their ground work whilst another pair were transferred to future courses at the School. Adverse weather conditions had played hell with the training syllabus and so a decision had been taken to extend No.44 Course by a week.

Although recent months had seen either zero or very few flying accidents at Morpeth, no less than four incidents were recorded for November 1943. Three of these involved engine failure. On the 13th, a Martinet target tug crashed just outside the RAF Morpeth airfield boundary due to its engine cutting out shortly after take-off. Neither the pilot, Flight Sergeant Pearch, or his Target Towing Officer, Leading Aircraftsman Osner, were injured although both men were taken to Station Sick Quarters to be examined. An Anson was also damaged on the 26th when its undercarriage collapsed just before the aircraft took off. Flown by Flight Sergeant Barnard, none of the five onboard (the pilot, an instructor and three cadets) were injured.

One point of note was that the last Botha finally left Morpeth that month for Abbotsinch (now Glasgow Airport) and a date with the scrapman's axe. On one of the ferry flights, both engines on the Botha had failed, and only quick thinking and experience on behalf of the pilot, Flying Officer Ilott, had saved the aircraft from being a total loss, although he was forced to land the machine in a field. Despite the type being universally hated across the RAF as a whole, some of the Polish pilots at Morpeth had reportedly developed a strange fondness for the Botha and were actually sad to see them go. Some of the unit's Ansons that were fitted with just one machine gun were also exchanged for machines that carried two. This finally ensured that Morpeth had received its permanent allocation of aircraft.

Flying Officer Marshall had been in charge of No.45 Course, aided by instructors Warrant Officers Slocombe, Sanders and Lown, plus Flight Sergeant Wymer and Sergeant Adams. It passed out on 11th December, with 53 out of an original 62 pupils passing, and was immediately replaced by No.49 Course, which had Polish, Dutch and Norwegian cadets as part of the intake. No.46 Course was led by Flight Lieutenant Robson, who was ably assisted by instructors Warrant Officer Robinson, Flight Sergeants Barnes and

Morrison, and Sergeant H. K. Williams. It passed out on 18th December 1943, with 54 passing, ten less than had started. No.50 Course arrived on the same day to ensure no gap in the training programme. Seven Free French and four Norwegians were among its numbers.

No.53 (Elementary Air Gunners) Course also began at Morpeth on 18th December 1943. This intake arrived direct from No.14 Initial Training Wing at Bridlington, and the 60 cadets involved were to receive four weeks' worth of elementary air gunners training at the Northumberland station.

One of the School's Martinets was lost on 22nd December 1943 when HP131 crashed near Stannington Mental Hospital. The pilot, Sgt. T. O. Anderson, was returning to Morpeth after a one hour ten minute-long flight, which involving towing a drogue target back and forth over the Druridge Bay ranges. Flying at an altitude of around 400 feet on the approach to the aerodrome, the reduction gear fitted to the aircraft's Bristol Mercury Mk.XXX engine suddenly failed. This piece of equipment acted as a regulator, lowering the power directed from the engine down to a level which the propeller could safely handle, without it over-speeding. With this safety feature removed, the Martinet's propeller detached and fell away, Anderson's view forward quickly being obscured by clouds of thick smoke pouring out of the dying engine. Unable to see where he was going and flying far too low to bail out of his stricken aircraft, Sgt. Anderson had no alternative but to stay at the controls and hope he survived the inevitable crash-landing.

At 1645 hours on the 22nd, Anderson's Martinet crashed into a wooded area about a mile south-east of Morpeth aerodrome. The aircraft was damaged beyond repair. According to the Station Medical Officer, the pilot had received a transverse 1½ inch cut on his forehead but was otherwise unscathed. The cut had to be sutured and therefore he was detained at Station Sick Quarters for 24 hours. The investigation confirmed that Anderson was in no way responsible for the incident and the subsequent loss of the Martinet. The most likely cause was put down to being a faulty ball bearing within the reduction gear. Such a small item had possibly caused the propeller to depart from the airframe. The aircraft was officially struck from RAF charge nine days later, having amassed a total of 257 flying hours whilst in service with No.4 Air Gunners School. It had been delivered to the unit from No.48 Maintenance Unit at Hawarden, Cheshire, on 14th December 1942, only a week after it was accepted from the factory.

The Martinets based at Morpeth carried the standard Training Command colour scheme, with a sky-blue rear fuselage band and an individual aircraft number in blue in front of the fuselage roundels. The Ansons used by No.4 Air Gunners School were mostly brand new aircraft, fitted with Bristol gun turrets and painted in the standard training scheme colours. On most of the aircraft, a single identifying letter was carried in blue behind the fuselage roundels, except for LV298, which wore a white "F".

December 1943 also saw major repairs being carried out on the runways and taxiways at Morpeth. Nineteen months of intensive operations had taken their toll on the surfaces and the work was urgently required since potholes and other damage was interfering with the smooth running of the training regime. Putting a main wheel into a large pothole could, in theory, have damaged the undercarriage assembly, caused propellers to strike the ground or the aircraft to turn unexpectedly. None of these actions were particularly desirable.

Avro Anson Mk.I K8838 became a ground instructional airframe with the maintenance serial 4426M, and it arrived at RAF Morpeth on 4th December 1943 for use by the instructors and trainees. This aircraft was struck off charge on 23rd January 1945, being surplus to requirements following the closure of No.4 Air Gunners School in December 1944, but that was still a year away.

CRISIS POINT: JANUARY-MARCH 1944

One of the old T1 hangar floors, pictured in March 2002. Note the old car lying on its side in the background, evidence of the "banger" races that used to occur at the site on an ad hoc basis back then. The fence has since been removed and the posts sawn off at their bases. The line where the door runnels are situated can be clearly seen. (Author)

No.47 Course passed out on New Year's Day 1944. 66 cadets had originally started the course and just seven failed to make the grade. Each pupil had received an average of 14 hours 20 minutes flying time and their average score was 77.8%. Only 1,000 flying hours had been achieved in total during December 1943, so this figure was all the more impressive for that. It had been calculated using the new accounting method of ignoring flight time to and from the ranges ("unproductive time"). Using the old scheme, the figure would have been in the region of 1,200 hours. No.51 Course, comprising Polish and Dutch personnel, arrived at Morpeth the same day.

No.48 Course passed out on 15th January and was immediately replaced by the cadets from No.52 Course, Canadians who had previously gone through the four week-long No.53 Elementary Air Gunners Course that began at Morpeth on 18th December 1943 and concluded on 15th January 1944. The latter therefore went straight from their elementary training to the real thing and were then joined by 15 cadets from an Initial Training Wing at Bridgnorth. No.48 Course had comprised no less than 70 cadets, which was a School record. 62 of them passed, one of which was recommended for a commission.

January 1944 had been another relatively good month in terms of total flying hours, aided by a healthy amount of unseasonably good weather. This allowed some 1,086 hours to be flown by the School, which was more than double the figure recorded for the same month in 1943. It was also recorded that twice the number of machine gun rounds had been fired as in January 1943 and nearly twice as much cine film exposed. Only one accident had been reported in January 1944 and it was a minor event, one which the station would not have even mentioned under an earlier system of accounting. The School had increased its hours of night flying although this was hampered by no less than eight pilots being posted away from the unit during the month. Four were British, and only three were posted in to replace them and the other four lost to the School. It was stated that No.4 Air Gunners School was running seriously short of British officers experienced in gunnery training flying duties.

Although there had been plenty of incidents involving aircraft from No.4 air Gunners School in 1942 and 1943, things reached a crisis point in February 1944 with seven separate accidents being recorded. This was the worst month in the unit's history, although none appear to have been sufficiently serious enough to warrant the aircraft involved being written off due to damage or crashes. Most of the machines involved must therefore have been repaired on site. Part of the reason for the increased accident rate may have been a new system of recording such events. This was reflected in the official station records although no punches were pulled when it came to assigning blame for some of them:

"The new system of accident reporting is partially the cause of the high figure which will give us the worst accident rate since the first month flying was carried out at this Unit. Four were taxying accidents, a serious reflection on the pilots. Steps are being taken to obviate a recurrence of this bad record."

Something had to be done about this situation as it was clearly interfering with the training programme. A Flying Control Officer, Flight Lieutenant D. H. Sinclair, was therefore posted in on the 12th to serve at the station. In our current safety-conscious age, it seems surprising that flying had taken place for 22 months before the lack of proper control of the landing circuit at Morpeth was addressed. It is even more surprising when one learns that a Flying Control building (what we would now refer to as a control tower) had existed there since August 1943. The aerodrome had a "bungalow-type" Watch Office, which was a 36-feet long Nissen hut fitted with two or possibly three bay windows. No.6007 Airfield Construction Squadron was responsible for these later additions to the building, which improved visibility for the staff looking after aircraft in the circuit at Morpeth.

No.49 Course passed out on 5th February and was replaced by the RAF, Free French and Belgian cadets of No.53 Course. A French Warrant Officer instructor was posted to Morpeth at the same time, presumably to assist with potential language barriers. 57 out of the original 63 pupils from No.49 Course managed to pass their final board exam and become trained air gunners.

No.50 Course ended on the 19th and 56 cadets from the 61 who began training, passed out successfully. No.54 Course, which was made up of British, Free French, Canadian and Polish personnel, turned up at Morpeth on the same day. During February 1944, three former pupils who had moved onto operational squadrons were awarded the Distinguished Flying Medal, the "other ranks" equivalent of the Distinguished Flying Cross given to those who demonstrated *"exceptional valour, courage or devotion to duty whilst flying in active operations against the enemy"*.

In addition to the lack of proper flying control at the station, the weather conspired to disrupt the training programme too, although 1,071 hours were recorded in February 1944, and this was 40 hours in excess of what had been notched up a year earlier.

February 1944 did however see a notable "first" at Morpeth as it saw a truly magnificent event which could so easily have ended in disaster for all involved. The station records take up the story:

"Extra Oval type of Blister Hangar moved without dismantling from one site to another – a distance of approximately ½ mile – movement was successful. As the work was in the nature of an experiment and it is not yet completed, no further comments are made – a full report will be rendered at a later date."

Although the blister type hangars dotted about Morpeth and other RAF stations were regarded as temporary structures, once erected they were usually there to stay. On the odd previous occasion that one had to be moved, the building was dismantled, moved and then re-erected, which of course involved a huge amount of both time and manpower. As the structure concerned in this "experiment" is referred to as an "Extra Oval" [sic], it was one of the three Miskins Extra Over blister hangars. Eight more blisters would be moved at Morpeth before the year was out.

The Morpeth WAAFs were extremely busy during February 1944 as they decorated and prepared their quarters for the forthcoming competition for best turned out buildings. This was a WAAF-only event and personnel at Morpeth competed against other stations across Flying Training Command. RAF officers and other ranks volunteered their time to help out where necessary. The cost of re-decorating the WAAF Dining Hall and Institute was covered by their own funds and used RAF labour, work being done outside duty hours. Judging was to take place the following month.

Re-decorating and tidying up would have probably happened elsewhere on the station in advance of Air Chief Marshal Sir Edgar Ludlow-Hewitt's official visit on 22nd February 1944. The Inspector-General of the RAF, he was accompanied by Wing Commander Dennison. Sir Edgar arrived the day before and spent the night at the station before his official inspection on the 22nd. He left by air at 1230 hours.

The station records for February 1944 also include a breakdown of the entire permanent staff based at RAF Morpeth:

RAF	706
WAAF	357
RAF Regiment	2
Army	1
Royal New Zealand Air Force	1
Royal Canadian Air Force	9
Royal Australian Air Force	23
Royal Netherlands Air Force	1
Total	1100

Out of the 246 cadets present when the survey was performed, there were 165 from the RAF, 4 Canadians, 18 Australians, 4 Dutch, one Belgian and 54 Free French.

Whilst the flying accidents that occurred at Morpeth were not listed in the official station record summaries, another incident was. On 1st February, one of No.4 Air Gunners School's Martinet target tugs force landed near Amble, presumably due to engine failure. The pilot, Flying Officer Newall, was unhurt, although he and his Target Towing Officer were taken to Station Sick Quarters at Acklington under the new arrangements for the Amble detachment.

Whilst personnel at the station were not specifically trained in the recovery of crashed aircraft and casualties, the proximity of Morpeth aerodrome to the Cheviot and Simonside Hills meant that they were often called out to assist or deal with incidents that occurred on high ground in Northumberland. In 1944, No.83

Maintenance Unit at Woolsington was nominally in charge of recoveries over much of northern England, at least north of the main Penrith to Darlington road but including the Lake District. This obviously kept their own staff incredibly busy and therefore Morpeth was often called upon to help out.

One such call-out occurred late into the evening of 3rd March 1944. A Lancaster from No.1666 Heavy Conversion Unit, based at RAF Wombleton on the edge of the North Yorkshire Moors, had already been listed as missing somewhere over the Cheviots. Lancaster Mk.I DS650/ND-P, flown by a Canadian pilot, Pilot Officer R. G. Calder, had taken off from Wombleton at 1845 hours on a "Bullseye" night navigation training flight. Not only was Calder and his new crew being tested, but so were the local air defences, as part of the exercise involving attacking simulated targets throughout the north of England.

At around 2200 hours that evening, Richard Dunn, a forestry worker living at Low Byrness, some five or six miles north-west of Otterburn, suddenly heard the noise of a large aircraft, one which sounded as though it was in a steep dive. Rushing outside his house, Dunn heard a fantastic roar and saw a four-engined bomber flying straight towards him at a very low level. He noticed that one of its engines was on fire and the airframe was shedding pieces as it flew north-westwards along Redesdale. Narrowly missing his house and others along the valley towards the village, he watched as it also managed to avoid hitting the nearby Byrness Hotel, located on the opposite side of the A68 before crashing into the hillside above and behind the building.

Richard Dunn had not been the only local resident to see the stricken bomber, and the alarm was soon raised. It was a frosty night, and the personnel dispatched from Morpeth did not reach the site until the early hours of the morning so could do little whilst it was still dark. These included the Senior Medical Officer and a single ambulance from the station. However, the would-be rescue party ended up searching for the bodies of five of the seven crew members, as only two were found in the main area of wreckage. Given the line of debris that lay in a reasonably straight line along the valley, it was assumed that Calder's Lancaster had broken up in mid-air during its final few moments. Dunn's report of pieces coming off the aircraft supported this view. Personnel from Morpeth finally found part of the bomber's tail unit, including one of the fins, some two and a half miles south-west of the main point of impact. Three bodies were discovered next to The Inkpots, a pair of houses about a mile down the valley from Byrness, and a fourth even closer to the village. The seventh airman was not found straight away but was located a day or two later.

Information provided by the Morpeth rescue and recovery party would have been used in the Heavy Conversion Unit's initial enquiry into the crash. The report into the incident stated that Pilot Officer Calder had in all likelihood lost control of his aircraft, whereupon it had entered a dive. The descent had become so steep that the Lancaster's speed increased beyond the airframe's tolerance levels, causing part of the tailplane to depart. Structural failure of the tail assembly, often involving the loss of fabric covering the elevators, was a known occurrence. However, some witnesses stated they had heard or observed "gun fire". This suggested that the bomber had either been attacked by an RAF night-fighter in error, or gunners at the nearby Otterburn and Redesdale Camps had opened fire on the aircraft. However, neither of these theories have ever been proven. The recovery party sent from Morpeth, possibly with the assistance of local farmers, brought as much of the wreckage that could be moved, down to the main road near Cottonshope. The pile of debris lay there for many years before finally being removed. Just south of Blakehopeburnhaugh, the section of tail unit was not recovered and remained where it had fallen until the 1960s when it disappeared.

According to the station records, March was a successful month:

"March 1944 was a most successful month for flying at Morpeth. 1,887 hours were flown with four accidents, two of which were unavoidable from the pilot's point of view. The weather was good for the time of year and 143.8% of the minimum pupil exercise commitment was carried out. There were 10.8% failures in exercises which was a considerable improvement on February."

No.51 Course passed out on 4th March. 55 from the original 61 cadets successfully completed the course. One was recommended for a commission and was promoted to Pilot Officer (this of course did not mean he was a pilot as it was merely a rank title). No.55 Course, comprising RAF Volunteer Reserve, Polish, Free French and Norwegian personnel, arrived at Morpeth the same day.

The following day, Group Captain Fear attended an Air Training Corps Rally at Newcastle Wing Headquarters. The cadets were being inspected and addressed by Air Marshal Sir E. L. Gossage, who was Chief Commandant and Director General of the Air Training Corps.

Group Captain A. M. Bentley, Officer Commanding RAF Eshott, arrived for a visit on the 10th. Although the exact purpose of this is not known, it is likely that the subject of No.57 Operational Training Unit's Advanced Flight at Boulmer came up. It had previously been arranged that some of the more proficient pupils, together with their instructors, would carry out dummy attacks on the Anson training aircraft when they were flying in the vicinity. This provided the gunnery cadets with much more realistic targets than drogues, although live ammunition obviously could not be fired!

On 14th March 1944, Squadron Leader D. A. Nicholls, the Officer Commanding Flying at Morpeth, was posted to No.5 (Pilot) Advanced Flying Unit at Ternhill in Shropshire. He was temporarily replaced by Flight Lieutenant F. T. Roberts, a most capable pilot who filled in until the arrival of Squadron Leader E. J. Ashby at the end of the month. The new Officer Commanding Flying no doubt had to deal with paperwork generated by the crash of a Martinet near Acklington at around 1700 hours on the same day. Both crew members were checked over by the Medical Officer at Acklington. Pilot Officer Kocot received minor injuries, including a lacerated left eyebrow, but he was judged fit enough to be returned to his unit. Aircraftsman First Class Clark, Kocot's Target Towing Operator, was less fortunate. He sustained a Colles fracture to his left wrist and had to be admitted to Station Sick Quarters at Acklington for treatment. Clark was discharged four days later.

The sole surviving Miskins Double Extra Over blister hangar at Morpeth, pictured in November 2021. Nine similar structures were moved around the aerodrome during 1944 without dismantling them first. Two were also destroyed in a gale in November that year. T-irons were the only forms of attachment to the ground used by the Miskins buildings so it is not really surprising that extremely strong winds would make them vulnerable to overturning. (Author)

18th March saw No.52 Course pass out, with just 59 out of the original intake of 67 completing the course. A single cadet was commissioned to the rank of Pilot Officer. This course was replaced by No.56 Course on the same day, the new intake being made up of British, Canadian, Free French, Belgian and Norwegian cadets.

The instruction staff changed during March with the departure of Flight Lieutenant W. H. Smith as commander of the Training Wing at Morpeth. He was replaced by Squadron Leader Storey on the 29th, who arrived from Headquarters, Flying Training Command. Flight Lieutenant G. E. Skinner turned up on the 18th to take up the duty of Senior Gunnery Officer, replacing Flight Lieutenant Robson.

Skinner had previously served at No.8 Air Gunners School at Evanton, north of Inverness. Robson was posted there to replace him. Morpeth also lost the services of Pilot Officer Milburn, one of the gunnery instructors, who was posted elsewhere on the 25th.

Two more Blister hangars were moved across the airfield during March 1944 without dismantling them first. They were relocated to more suitable sites. A report, together with photographs of the two moves, was submitted to Headquarters, Flying Training Command and No.29 (Training) Group Headquarters for their perusal. The hangar moves must have been a sight to behold.

Squadron Officer Lady A. I. Seton from No.29 (Training) Group, accompanied by Squadron Leader Fenwick, arrived at Morpeth on the 23rd to inspect the efforts made by the WAAFs and other station personnel to decorate their buildings for the preliminary stage of Flying Training Command's WAAF Quarters Competition.

A second Martinet was involved in an accident on the 26th when one crashed about a mile beyond the Runway 11 threshold at about 1515 hours. Flight Sergeant Tatham was at the controls and suffered engine failure as he was climbing away from the airfield. He was suffering from shock and was kept under observation for 24 hours before being released. Corporal Whatmough, his Target Towing Operator, was unharmed in the incident.

An ambulance with Morpeth's Medical Officer onboard was sent to the scene of a crash near Alnmouth on the same day. A Hawker Typhoon fighter-bomber from one of the squadrons based across at Acklington had come to grief there. However, when the vehicle arrived at the crash site, one dispatched from Acklington had got there first so the Morpeth ambulance was not required.

HERE COME THE "HEAVIES": APRIL-JUNE 1944

April 1944 was not a good month for training as no less than 13 days were lost due to bad weather, visibility dropping to less than 1,000 yards during the bulk of that period. However, strenuous efforts to maximise and even increase flying hours on the days when flying could take place allowed No.4 Air Gunners School to maintain its flying commitment for the month. The total flying time for April was recorded as 1,499 hours 25 minutes.

57 cadets out of the original 63 starting on No.53 Course were able to pass on 1st April 1944, and that was no April Fool. On the same day, No.57 Course arrived at Morpeth, made up of British, Polish and Belgian trainees.

No.54 Course passed out on the 15th, with just 53 out of the 64 that began their training managing to pass the final board exam. However, those that did pass out had achieved a 78.1% score which was extremely high. They were replaced by No.58 Course, which comprised British and Free French cadets.

18th April saw a much larger and heavier aircraft arrive at RAF Morpeth. An American B-17 Flying Fortress arrived that evening, its approach starting some six or seven miles out from the aerodrome. The pilot no doubt wanted to make doubly sure of his landing, since the runways at Morpeth were rather short for bomber operations. The B-17 was carrying an officer, Captain B. Markoff of the United States Army Air Force, who gave a talk on Anglo-American relations, one that was reportedly well received by all present. The bomber took off again at lunchtime the next day, making a low pass over RAF Morpeth as he departed. Jack Thompson witnessed this from Morpeth School, which he was attending at the time.

RAF Morpeth assumed responsibility for looking after Usworth airfield near Sunderland (now the site of the Nissan car plant) on the 21st. It was now RAF Usworth's "parent station" as the latter had been placed into what was termed "Care and Maintenance", essentially a mothballing operation pending a decision as to either dispose of the site or reactivate it at some point in the future. There were still around 160 personnel stationed at Usworth, although they were awaiting news of postings elsewhere so were unable to give much assistance to the 21 Morpeth staff who were tasked with looking after the station – one officer and 20 other ranks. Back at Morpeth, three more Blister hangars were successfully moved in April 1944 without being dismantled first, to what were termed in the official records as *"more beneficial sites"*.

On the 22nd, it was No.59 Course's turn to pass out. Another 53 cadets successfully navigated the final hurdle, 62 having begun the course. The successful gunners' accuracy was lower, at 73.2%, but this was well within acceptable limits. No.59 Course, made up solely of RAF personnel, arrived at Morpeth the same day. By the end of the month, no less than 5,386 pupils had passed through Morpeth since it began training air gunners.

The Station Commander at RAF Morpeth, Group Captain Fear, replaced his personal transport, Avro Tutor K3256, with Miles Magister L8359 on 25th April 1944. This aircraft took up the civilian registration G-AKRH after the war was over. It was finally scrapped at Blackpool in 1963.

Two accidents occurred on the same day, the 30th, with both involving Martinets from No.4 Air Gunners School. One crash-landed in the vicinity of the aerodrome at around 1025 hours, with the pilot, Flight Sergeant Thomas, and the Target Towing Officer, Leading Aircraftsman Wilkinson, both suffering from slight shock. Neither required treatment at Station Sick Quarters. The second crash took place around 1745 hours when a Martinet also came down near the airfield. Sergeant Bentley and Aircraftsman First Class Logan survived the event without injury.

No.4 Air Gunners School lost another Martinet, HP481, when it crashed on 1st May 1944. The aircraft force-landed near Ulgham Grange at around 0935 hours, injuring both the pilot, Sergeant Bisanz, and the Target Towing Operator, Leading Aircraftsman Fitzgerald. Both sustained head injuries in the incident and were also suffering from shock. They were taken to Ashington General Hospital for treatment.

No.56 Course completed its training on the 5th, when 63 out of the original 67 starters passed the final board exam. This was quite an achievement, and their average percentage score was 78.5%, a very high amount compared to most. No.60 Course, comprised of British, Polish, Free French and Norwegians, turned up to start their own gunnery training the same day.

Another Blister hangar was moved to a different location on the airfield during May, and on this occasion a cine film was taken of proceedings. This slowed down the operation due to the filming, but the move was completely successful. Out of the nine hangars that were planned to be moved, seven had now been relocated.

Celebrations for the anniversary of the formation of the WAAF were in planning, and RAF Morpeth had not been forgotten in terms of local arrangements, as the official station records stated:

"A conference was held at No.3 Balloon Centre Longbenton on 12/5/44 of WAAF representatives of local Units, also a number of Station Administrative Officers to decide on arrangements for the celebration of the Anniversary of the formation of the WAAF in the city of Newcastle. It was decided that such celebrations would be held on Sunday 2/7/44, consisting of a march past of approximately 850 WAAFs, service in the Cathedral, tea, and if possible an all WAAF entertainment in the evening. Longbenton to make all detailed arrangements. RAF Station Morpeth to provide 100 airwomen for the celebration. This is additional to any individual arrangements made by Units for their own WAAF. Flight Officer Q. E. Bee (Officer Commanding, WAAF) and Squadron Leader Cradock attended the conference."

On the 22nd, a meeting was held at Morpeth to discuss the above and the station's own celebrations. It was decided that a march past would be held by all WAAF personnel, followed by a special tea. There would also be side shows and a dance at the WAAF communal site during the evening.

No.57 Course was not as successful as the earlier one that month as just 53 from an intake of 61 passed the final exam on 20th May 1944. They were immediately replaced by No.61 Course, drawn from RAF personnel only, plus a Pool of gunners who arrived on the same day.

On 24th May, a Vickers Wellington bomber from RAF Moreton-in-the-Marsh force-landed near Blyth at around 1300 hours. An ambulance and medical staff from Morpeth attended the incident but the six crewmen onboard the training aircraft were uninjured and were returned to their unit the same day. The amount of damage sustained by the aircraft and its identity are not known.

Another Martinet suffered damage in a force-landing some three miles north-east of RAF Morpeth at 1130 hours on the 28th. The pilot, Flight Sergeant Burdass, was uninjured in the incident.

May 1944 saw a record number of flying hours carried out by No.4 Air Gunners School. It entailed a huge amount of extra work from maintenance staff to ensure that enough aircraft were ready for training flights, but also plenty of organisational skills behind the scenes from station staff, down to even mundane matters such as changing shifts at short notice and having meals ready at different times of the day. All this had been achieved despite days where the weather intervened and disrupted the flying programme.

No.58 Course ended on 3rd June 1944 with 57 cadets completing their training successfully. Only five had failed to make the grade. They were replaced by No.62 Course, which was comprised of RAF, Dutch and Free French personnel.

Jack Thompson remembers flying from Morpeth on 8th June 1944 in Airspeed Oxford X7262, this aircraft belonging to the Station Flight at RAF Halton. The aircraft had flown up to Morpeth for the express intention of giving Air Training Corps cadets valuable air experience flights. 35 cadets from No.404 (Morpeth) Squadron and No.1000 (Bedlington) Squadron were given anywhere between 20 and 30 minutes in the air. Nearly four hours were flown in total, and the aircraft stayed a further day, although it was unserviceable on the 9th and another two flights scheduled for that day had to be cancelled at short notice. The first cadets to attend the annual summer camp arrived on the 18th.

The trainee gunners at Morpeth obtained a close look at an actual operational bomber on the morning of 9th June 1944 when Lancaster Mk.III BM597 from No.463 Squadron landed there after a raid on Rennes, having been forced to divert away from its base at Waddington in Lincolnshire due to bad weather. Other aircraft from the same unit landed at RAF Acklington as well that morning. The Australian pilot of the "Lanc", Pilot Officer A. B. Tottenham, rang Acklington to find out the planned take-off time of his colleagues, so he could fly back to his home base with them! According to Jack Thompson, who saw the aircraft at Morpeth, Tottenham was happy for him to look over the Lancaster, but he was prevented from doing so by station personnel.

No.59 Course passed out on the 10th, with 56 out of an original 61 starters getting through their final board exam. The average accuracy was 77.8%, a really good achievement. Replacements in the shape of No.63 Course and another pool of gunners arrived at Morpeth on the same day. French and Czech trainees were among their numbers. It was also reported that no less than 14 ex-trainees had received the Distinguished Flying Medal between 19th May and 2nd June, which presumably was a good morale builder for those attending Morpeth at the time.

The final Blister hangars were moved during the month, proving that these structures could be successfully relocated without having to dismantle them first. Two of the Double Extra Over blisters were to have their ends filled in using metal and wooden walls, whilst the others were to be fitted with canvas curtains. All work was to be carried out by station personnel.

At around 1220 hours on the 16th, Spitfire Mk.I N3052 from No.57 Operational Training Unit at RAF Eshott force-landed at Hepscott Red House, just over a mile south-east of Morpeth town centre. News of the incident reached Station Sick Quarters at Morpeth just five minutes later and medical personnel from the station attended the scene. The pilot, Sergeant B. Storaas, strained back muscles in the incident and was dispatched to Eshott via ambulance for treatment.

Medical staff from Morpeth were also sent to the scene of another air crash involving aircraft based elsewhere. At around 1730 hours on the 19th, Station Sick Quarters were informed by the Duty Pilot that parachutes had been seen descending north-west of the airfield. An ambulance was dispatched immediately and soon arrived at the site of a mid-air collision involving Spitfire Mk.I R7065 from No.57 Operational Training Unit at Eshott and Bristol Beaufort Mk.I W6540 from No.54 Operational Training Unit at Charter Hall, near Coldstream. The two machines had collided over Rayburn Lake, the Beaufort coming down on Wingates Moor whilst the Spitfire crashed near the village of Netherwitton. The official records list the Beaufort as a Beaufighter (a different aircraft built by the same manufacturer). The pilot and observer of the Beaufort managed to bail out of their stricken aircraft, and these were indeed the parachutes that were observed. The pilot of the Spitfire, Sergeant D. C. Mitchell, an instructor at Eshott, was killed. He had served with No.65 Squadron from August 1940 until the middle of 1941 when he moved to North Africa. Mitchell had returned to the UK by the beginning of 1944. An ambulance from Eshott had already reached the site before the Morpeth vehicle arrived, and therefore the latter was not required.

All of the organisational work in advance of the Ceremonial Parade for the WAAF Birthday Celebrations arranged for 2nd July were suddenly cancelled during June. However, on 28th June 1944, RAF Morpeth celebrated the event with a march past, short open air service, tea and dance. Members of the local press were invited to attend, and photographs were taken of the event. The following day's Evening Chronicle newspaper carried details of proceedings but not the name of the RAF station involved for security reasons:

ANNIVERSARY OF THE W.A.A.F.

JUNE 28th, 1944.

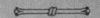

14·00 hrs.   **TEA**

BIRTHDAY CAKE.

COLD HAM AND TONGUE.

ASSORTED SALADS.

BREAD AND BUTTER.

BLACKBERRY JAM.

ASSORTED CAKES.

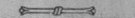

18·30 hrs.   **ENTERTAINMENTS.**

FUN FAIR.

ALL THE FUN OF THE FAIR.

ROLL 'EM.

20·30 hrs.   **FANCY DRESS BALL.**

ALL AND SUNDRY.

GIVE US THE GEN.

"WAAFs Fifth Birthday Celebrations at North East Aerodrome

North Country girls took a big part in the fifth birthday celebrations of the WAAF at a North East Aerodrome.

One of them, Aircraftswomen Crosbie of Seaham Harbour, the junior WAAF among the 300 at the station, had the honour of cutting the three-tiered birthday cake, while another, Corporal Davis, whose parents live in Newcastle, had painted in oils a large portrait of a uniformed WAAF, which hung in the dining hall, and had also painted floral decorations on the wall.

The first part of the celebrations was formal with the Officer Commanding, Group Captain A. H. Fear, inspecting the girls as aircraft wheeled overhead, followed by a short service.

Aircraftswomen Crosbie cuts the three-tiered cake at the WAAF Fifth Birthday Celebrations held at RAF Morpeth on 28th June 1944.

Birthday Cake

Group Captain Fear then took the salute at a March Past.

Flying Officer Hicks, Catering Officer, and his staff of cooks had made a special effort for the party and the girls, all released from duty with the exception of those on essential jobs, sat down to a meal of cold ham, cold tongue and salad with tomatoes and eggs, and cream cakes.

The birthday cake was a work of art – iced in green, pink and white, and bearing model aeroplanes.

WAAF and RAF officers, including the Station Commander and his wife, waited on the girls at the table.

Music was supplied with the Durham Light Infantry band and later the RAF joined in a fancy dress ball in the dining hall."

One of the gunners attending Morpeth during May and June 1944 was Sgt. J. T. Brittain. His log book shows that he amassed a total of 30 hours 45 minutes flying time between 20th May and 19th June that year, spread over 34 separate flights. All of these were in the School's Anson aircraft. However, four of these flights ended without any actual practice firing being carried out, either due to problems with the aircraft or the machine gun fitted in its turret. On his second day of practice firing over the coastal ranges, which involved three separate flights, one was scrubbed due to the magazine jamming. Sgt. Brittain would experience this on two further occasions. Three days later, on 24th May, one of the engine cowlings fitted to Anson LT430/K came loose so the pilot, Flying Officer Girard, had to return to base thirty minutes after departure. This meant that Brittain had to wait a further two days before he could complete that particular task in his training schedule. However, despite the failures in the equipment, he eventually passed the course with an 86.5% rating. Squadron Leader Storey, Officer Commanding, Training Wing at No.4 Air Gunners School, commented that Brittain was *"a keen, hard worker, will make a very capable air gunner."*

After going through two different Operational Training Units, Sgt. Brittain was posted to No.1653 Heavy Conversion Unit at Chedburgh and then RAF North Luffenham, clocking up nearly 40 hours in the Stirling Mk.IIIs and Lancaster Mk.Is used there for conversion training. He finally joined No.195 Squadron at Wrattling Common on 3rd February 1945 and became a member of Warrant

Officer Brown's crew, flying on at least 11 separate bombing raids before the end of the war. His experience showed that even after passing the course at Morpeth in June 1944, it may have been seven or eight months before a newly-qualified gunner would participate in a bombing raid. Earlier in the war, some Operational Training Unit crews who were considered to be more adept than others, were allowed to participate in the "Thousand Bomber Raids" over Germany, in order that the required numbers of aircraft was reached.

AN INFLUX OF ITALIANS: JULY-SEPTEMBER 1944

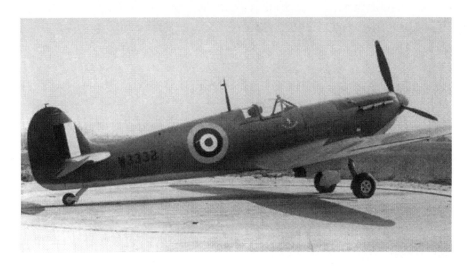

Spitfire Mk.VB W3332 was an almost identical machine to EP110 which crashed near RAF Morpeth on 12th August 1944. The aircraft came from No.57 Operational Training Unit at Eshott, about five miles north of the town. (Unknown)

The training never seemed to cease at Morpeth. No.60 Course ended on 1st July 1944 with the impressive average accuracy score of 78.4%, 61 cadets out of an original intake of 64 passing the final board exam. British, French and Polish pupils belonging to No.65 Course turned up on the same day to begin their own training.

Another VIP arrived at Morpeth onboard a Beech Expeditor on 5th July 1944. This was the Marshal of the RAF, Sir John Salmon, who watched a large parade consisting of officers, enlisted airmen and WAAFs from the station, plus air cadets from various Newcastle units and No.1431 (Newbiggin) Squadron. The parade was held near the main gate, next to the gunnery workshops located adjacent to the Saltwick to Mitford road. Sir John's aircraft was hangared in a nearby T1 shed whilst he attended the event. Again, photographs of the event were taken.

On 15th July, No.61 Course passed out, with 55 successful cadets out of an original 62. They achieved the exact same accuracy score as the previous group. No.66 Course, which replaced them, was significant as among its number were Icelandic and Persian cadets. The Persian candidate was Lieutenant A. Pur Ansari, who eventually was posted to No.1 Radio School at RAF Cranwell, Bedfordshire, after completing his course in September 1944. Bad weather during early July had affected both of the courses that ended that month, although clearly this had not had too much of an effect on matters.

In mid-July 1944, a group of 25 Italian prisoners of war arrived at RAF Morpeth and began work in a variety of non-operational roles. Although the Geneva Convention forbade the use of POWs as forced labour, the Italians volunteered their services as they had freely decided to co-operate with the British authorities. They were therefore officially referred to as "Italian Co-operators". In September 1943, following the Italian armistice, the country had split into two, the northern half becoming the fascist Salo Republic, allied to the Germans, and the southern part of Italy sided with the Allies. Two wooden huts located on the western side of the aerodrome, surplus to requirements for both the RAF and WAAF, were used to accommodate some of the Italians, but others were brought to the station from camps located elsewhere in the area. Some of these men decided to stay in Britain after the war. Whilst at RAF Morpeth, they carried out a range of often menial tasks but showed a keenness to work and it was hoped that they would prove very useful.

No.62 Course was completed on 29th July with 59 trainees out of an original 63 successfully passing the final hurdle. A pool of Czech, Dutch, Free French and Polish trainee gunners replaced them. This may have been due to manpower shortages, which were beginning to show in all of the services at the time. Based at Morpeth since April 1943, No.6207 (Bomb Disposal) Flight left the station for North Weald in Essex. This may have been connected with the onslaught of new V-weapons which began in June 1944.

On 11th August, No.63 Course ended with 57 cadets out of 64 passing out. This lower number of successful trainees was reflected in the reduced accuracy average, just 67.3% being recorded. No.67 Course turned up the following day, comprised of British, Czech, Dutch, Free French and Polish trainees.

Group Captain F. W. Hall arrived from No.8 Air Gunners School, RAF Evanton, on 12th August 1944 prior to taking over as Morpeth's station commander. Such appointments always involved a few days where the old and new commanding officers worked together to ensure a seamless handover. Hall officially took over on the 16th, with Group Captain Fear going onto what was known as the Special Duties List. This was a nominal "unit" for personnel who would go onto serve at or command RAF organisations which were not often recognised as such and avoided staff officers being "left in limbo", administratively speaking.

Also on the 12th, a message was received at the station at about 1030 hours to say that a Spitfire had crashed three miles south-west of the airfield. The aircraft, EP110, belonged to No.57 Operational Training Unit at RAF Eshott and was being flown by Flying Officer Osborne when it struck power cables which caused the engine to fail. An ambulance was dispatched from Morpeth and picked up the pilot, who was declared to be uninjured. He was transported to RAF Eshott for further medical checks at that station's Sick Quarters.

The 15th saw the cancellation of the planned station parade to commemorate the Battle of Britain. This was due to bad weather, which also plagued the flying programme for the entire month and as a result, *"training didn't come up to expectations."*

Another Martinet force-landed near the town of Morpeth on the 16th. Flight Sergeant Thomas, who had already survived one similar event, came through another such incident without apparent harm at first, although he was quickly admitted to Station Sick Quarters suffering from pneumonitis. Leading Aircraftsman Warner, the Target Towing Operator, was unscathed. The Martinet came down about a mile east of the town centre, on the northern side of the River Wansbeck.

Better results in terms of numbers of successful cadets occurred when No.64 Course sat their final exams on 25th August. 59 cadets from an original intake of 63 made the grade. The trainees assigned to No.68 Course arrived at Morpeth on the 26th, together with pool members that included Dutch and Free French among their ranks. The official records state that extremely bad flying weather was experienced throughout August 1944, with 179 hours being lost. However, some 1,717 hours were flown in total, so sterling efforts had been made to take advantage of the better days. Work on walls to seal off the ends of two Blister hangars was finally completed during the month as well.

No.65 Course passed out on 9th September 1944, with 54 cadets successfully completing the course out of an original intake of 61. Their passing out parade coincided with the visit by Air Commodore L. G. Croke, who was inspecting the station as part of his monthly visit. He took the opportunity to present the successful cadets with their brevets. In a change to normal practice, no replacement course turned up at RAF Morpeth that day. No.69 Course eventually arrived on the 16th with British, Belgian, Dutch, French and Polish trainees. They were joined by members of Pool No.9, who were British and Norwegian.

On the 23rd, 58 cadets from No.66 Course also passed out after completing their final exam. 61 had started so this was a fantastic result given the figures over the previous few months. No more intakes arrived at Morpeth that month to replace them. With only one full course turning up during September, was the writing finally on the wall for No.4 Air Gunners School?

SCALING DOWN: OCTOBER-DECEMBER 1944

The Towed Target Array building pictured in March 2002. Various types of towed drogue and flag targets were stored in this structure when not in use. It was the job of the Towed Target Operator in the Lysander and later Martinet tug aircraft to store the drogues after use. (Author)

The month of October began badly. A Martinet tipped up onto its nose on taking off from Morpeth at around 1030 hours on the 3rd. An ambulance was dispatched onto the airfield, but the pilot and Towed Target Operator were unharmed.

On the 6th, Anson Mk.I W2632 collided with another Anson, EF806 from No.62 Operational Training Unit at RAF Ouston, in the circuit at Morpeth. The Ouston-based aircraft was performing a blind approach and airborne intercept training flight and had been aloft for some twenty minutes.

Flying Officer F. Kurpiel was a trainee radio operator at No.62 Operational Training Unit, RAF Ouston. He was onboard Anson Mk.I EF806 when it collided with Anson W2632 from No.4 Air Gunners School over the western part of the landing circuit at Morpeth. Rather than being buried at St. Mary's in Morpeth, he was interred elsewhere, and his grave can be found at Chevington Cemetery near the former RAF Acklington airfield.

In W2632, the instructor pilot, Flight Sergeant E. W. Tranmere and his pupil, Warrant Officer J. E. Restell, were killed when their aircraft crashed at Higham Dykes near Ponteland following the mid-air collision. The pilot (F. A. Stevenson, rank unknown), instructor (Warrant Officer Woodward), and both of the trainees flying in Anson EF806 (Pilot Officer Collins and Flying Officer Kurpiel) were also killed in the incident. A Court of Inquiry was held at Morpeth on the 10th to determine the cause. This was followed up by the arrival on the 14th by Squadron Leader J. C. Hay of the Air Ministry's Accidents Branch.

However, despite this further tragedy, the numbers of crashes involving Ansons were much less than those involving Bothas. The serviceability of the Ansons was also much higher, leading to fewer engine failures and subsequent forced landings.

No.67 Course ended on 7th October 1944 with just one cadet failing to pass out of a total intake of 58 trainees. This was a really impressive result, although such gains would not be capitalised upon for reasons that became clear as the end of 1944 approached. It was the only one to finish training during the entire month. No.70 Course turned up at Morpeth on the same day, comprised of British, Belgian, Norwegian and Polish personnel. What was not appreciated by many at the time was that this would be the very last course to arrive for training by No.4 Air Gunners School.

A further Martinet tug was lost on 8th October 1944 when MS850 was forced to belly land in a field near Warkworth following engine failure. Altogether, some fifty-four different examples of this aircraft served with the training unit at Morpeth at various times during 1943 and 1944.

Life as a trainee air gunner at RAF Morpeth could occasionally be challenging: one pupil stated the following:

"(...) the flying part of the training was particularly enjoyable, though sometimes frightening depending on which pilot we had. The Anson had one turret and usually three trainee Gunners changed places in the aircraft depending on the particular exercise. The last into the turret generally sat with the pilot on take-off and

had to wind up the undercarriage: some three hundred winds, or so it seemed!"

The Anson was fitted with a manually retracted undercarriage, a hand crank being located in the cockpit. 140 turns were required to retract the undercarriage: it probably just seemed like three hundred to the unfortunate pupil. Being last on the crew roster therefore became rather unpopular among the gunnery pupils at the aerodrome.

According to Eric Taylor, the Bristol turrets fitted to the Ansons were designed to be equipped with two machine guns, but in his experience, they only had one fitted while at Morpeth. He remembered some of the duties he carried out there with the Air Training Corps:

"One of the duties we ATC cadets got was to remove every fifth round from the ammunition belts and replace it with a tracer bullet, so that the gunners could see where their shots were going. The belts were then rolled up and the tips of the bullets were painted — red, green, blue, etc., so that if the gunners managed to hit the drogue, the colours around the bullet hole would identify the gunner responsible."

Eric Taylor also managed to sit in on some of these lectures:

"Instructors were RAF NCOs with very little 'teacher training', I think. Many of the trainees were foreign, mainly French, and couldn't speak much English. Sometimes a trainee would act as interpreter, but I often wondered how much the audience took in. As a keen aircraft recognition enthusiast, I was pleased to attend some of the recognition classes. As many of the trainees would be gunners on bombers over enemy territory in a few weeks, their proficiency was interesting — some of them just didn't have a clue!"

By October 1944, the risk of invasion by the enemy was regarded as so slight that Morpeth's Station Defence Flight was disbanded and replaced by the formation of two training flights, both largely being made up from personnel who were earmarked for overseas postings. The anti-aircraft defences were left unchanged although it must have been recognised that the *Luftwaffe* was not capable of mounting any serious raids over Northumberland at that point in the war.

On 4th November 1944, an extremely strong gale uprooted two of the Miskins Blisters at Morpeth and lifted them into the air, dropping them upside-down and ensuring their total destruction. That would have been a frightening spectacle for anyone who was unfortunate enough to be close by at the time. These hangars did not require any foundations, simply being anchored by T-irons staked into the ground. Perhaps this is why the 1944 storm caused so much havoc. The Dorman Long type blister (4630/42) was constructed differently, made from RSJ-type arched ribs, the whole assembly being bolted to prepared foundations.

No.68 Course passed out the same day, with 55 cadets out of the original 58 managing to get through the final board exam. Those cadets who made the grade also managed to notch up an extremely impressive 79.5% average accuracy score. 415,400 rounds of 0.303-inch machine gun bullets were fired during the month of November and some 13,700 hours of cine film footage were developed. No replacement course arrived at Morpeth. Presumably Group Captain Hall had already been tipped off as to the School's impending fate.

Flight Lieutenant F. T. Roberts was one of the most experienced pilots at RAF Morpeth. On 2nd August 1944 he had been posted to No.1426 (Enemy Aircraft) Flight located at RAF Collyweston (now the western end of RAF Wittering). Together with an escort of Spitfires, he returned to Morpeth on 23rd November 1944 in the captured *Luftwaffe* Junkers Ju 88A-5 which wore the RAF serial number EE205 (*werke nummer* 3457) for a visit and demonstrated the aircraft over the aerodrome the following day. No.1426 Flight was making a film at Catterick at the time, and he had decided to visit his old mates up at Morpeth and show the trainees what a real enemy aircraft looked like.

Junkers Ju88A-5 werke number 3457 had worn the markings 4D+DL whilst in Luftwaffe service, being part of the 3rd Staffel of Kampfgeschwader 30 (3./KG30). It landed in error at Lulsgate Bottom (now Bristol Airport) on 24th July 1941 and was captured, becoming one of No.1426 (Enemy Aircraft) Flight's "circus" of enemy machine and allocated the RAF serial EE205. It visited Morpeth on 23rd November 1944 and was demonstrated over the airfield the following day. (Crown Copyright expired)

No.4 Air Gunners School was still processing air gunners courses throughout the year, but the impending end of the war in Europe and a rationalisation of the existing training structure meant that the School closed on 9th December 1944. No.69 Course passed out on the same day, with 58 out of the original intake of 64 trainees successfully becoming air gunners. No.70 Course was still underway when closure occurred, its 73 cadets being transferred to No.3 Air Gunners School across at RAF Castle Kennedy, near Stranraer.

The School had trained over four thousand air gunners at Morpeth since April 1942, its aircraft had flown over 37,000 hours and an estimated 12 million rounds of ammunition had been fired. Two of the School's Ansons transferred to No.3 Air Gunners School at Castle Kennedy, namely LV292 and MG415. As for the other aircraft, seven Ansons were sent to RAF Penhros in North Wales to serve with No.9 (Observer) Advanced Flying Unit. These were LT935, LV165, LV300, LV314, LV317, LV319 and MG110. LT490 and

LV161 were transferred to the Fleet Air Arm, while LT430 and MG106 ended up in France. A handful of others were transferred to other RAF units, but six of the Ansons had been struck from charge by the end of 1944 and four more had suffered the same fate by December 1945.

Some of the Martinets were passed to other Air Gunners Schools and at least one aircraft was passed across to No.9 (Observers) Advanced Flying Unit. The others were placed into storage and scrapped after the end of the war. Going into Christmas 1944, RAF Morpeth faced a somewhat uncertain future.

CARE & MAINTENANCE: WINTER 1944/1945

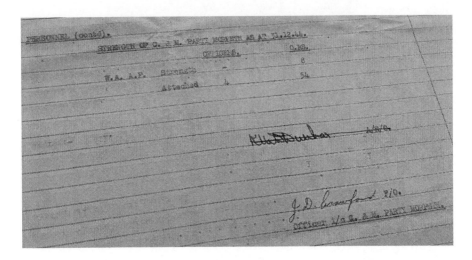

WAAFs made up part of the Care & Maintenance detail assigned to look after RAF Morpeth whilst it was essentially mothballed between December 1944 and April 1945. Flying Officer Crawford was in charge, his relatively lowly rank signifying the lack of priority the airfield was now receiving.

Following the closure of the station's only flying unit, RAF Morpeth was reduced to "Care and Maintenance" status, being looked after by a team of personnel stationed at RAF Woolsington (now Newcastle International Airport). According to a line entered in the official records, the changeover was recorded as follows:

"No.4 Air Gunners School closed, and Unit became C & M Party Morpeth".

The Care & Maintenance Party consisted of 12 officers and 28 other ranks, but a further 30 officers and 158 other ranks were also attached to the unit. 8 WAAF other ranks were also assigned, together with another 4 WAAF officers and 54 other ranks who had been temporarily attached to the Party. The whole unit was led by

Flying Officer J. D. Crawford, whose relatively junior officer rank demonstrated that the station was effectively being mothballed. If the war had ended over the winter of 1944/45, Morpeth may well have closed there and then, the fate of many airfields almost immediately after the surrender in May 1945.

Little occurred at Morpeth during the time it was under Care and Maintenance, although Wing Commander A. G. Wilson, Senior Medical Officer of No.29 (Training) Group stopped by to visit the station on 28th December 1944, staying overnight before returning to the Group's Headquarters across at Dumfries. There were no aircraft accidents to speak of during the time Morpeth was under Care & Maintenance as few if any machines were assigned to the station at this stage.

Work was done on a continuing basis to ensure that the aerodrome could be reactivated immediately if required by the war situation, but generally little was carried out beyond essential maintenance of the runways, taxiways and other important areas across the site. However, many of the buildings on the dispersed sites were simply left to rot as the staff were often busy dealing with more pressing tasks.

It looked as though Morpeth's war was over. Or was it?

THE FRENCH INVASION: APRIL-JULY 1945

Spitfire Mk.IX EN398 had been flown by the famous British fighter ace Johnnie Johnstone. It was one of the machines used by No.80 (French) Operational Training Unit at Morpeth in the summer of 1945. (Unknown)

Morpeth's enforced period of hibernation lasted until 23rd April 1945 when No.80 Operational Training Unit was formed there, coming under the control of No.12 (Fighter) Group. Its role was to convert French pilots from basic training aircraft to the Supermarine Spitfire. In late 1944, and with the end of the war in Europe in sight, French Air Marshal Valin ordered the famous French ace Christian Martell to establish an operational training unit in Britain for the exclusive use of French pilots. Following the end of their course at Morpeth, the pilots would then serve in the four French Spitfire squadrons attached to the Second Tactical Air Force.

The name "Christian Martell" was actually an alias to protect the Frenchman's real identity, Pierre Montet, and by extension his family. They were still living in Occupied France during the war, and if Montet's real name had been known, there was a possibility of German reprisals against them. Montet/"Martell" had joined the *Armee de l'Air* in October 1936. An exceptional pilot, once France had fallen in June 1940, he escaped to England and joined the Free French forces, serving with No.341 Squadron.

Like No.4 Air Gunners School, No.80 Operational Training Unit operated a mixture of aircraft. When initially established, it was assigned 24 Spitfire Mk.IXs, 14 Master Mk.IIs and four Martinet TT Mk.Is. The unit also had a de Havilland Dominie (the RAF version of the Dragon Rapide) as a transport. The ferry pilots of No.4 Aircraft Delivery Flight flew the Operational Training Unit's Spitfires to Morpeth direct from their previous owners, No.441 Squadron at RAF Digby, Lincolnshire, and also from their own base at RAF Clifton, near York. No.80 Operational Training Unit ended up "owning" one of Wing Commander Johnnie Johnson's previous mounts on strength, namely Spitfire Mk.IX EN398. He had shot down a reported sixteen enemy aircraft using this machine.

A small element from No.80 Operational Training Unit was soon established across at RAF Eshott, about six miles north of Morpeth town centre, which had hosted its own Spitfire training unit, No.57 Operational Training Unit, since November 1942. This detachment observed how Eshott's Operational Training Unit worked and received advice from the personnel stationed there, with the intention of putting what was learnt into practice back at Morpeth.

The French Operational Training Unit was the last flying unit to be based at RAF Morpeth; its stay was rather brief, however, as it moved across to RAF Ouston at the end of July 1945. Spitfire Mk.IXs from the unit noted at Morpeth during its short period of residence included BR140, BR600, BS247, BS403, MA476, MA528 and MA601.

The unit's commanding officer, "Christian Martel" was killed at Ouston on 31st August 1945, one month after the unit had moved there from Morpeth, when his Spitfire crashed after engine failure. Montet had been credited with seven confirmed kills and six "probables". He was awarded with the Legion de Honor, the Distinguished Flying Cross, and the American Silver Star in addition to other awards.

Very little is actually known about the activities of No.80 (French) Operational Training Unit and the official records, if these were retained in the UK, have not been traced.

August 1945 saw Morpeth aerodrome a much quieter place than it had been over the previous three and a half years. Most of the wartime station personnel had left the service or were waiting to do so, leaving only a small rump of people to keep essential functions and services running. The aerodrome itself was closed for flying purposes. However, despite this, the RAF had not quite finished using the site.

POST-WAR & CLOSURE

One of the large T1 hangars at Morpeth, pictured before its dismantling and removal by the local council in the early 1980s. In the post-war period the surviving shed-type hangars were used for storage, most notably "Green Goddess" fire engines in case of a national emergency. The hangar base is still visible along with the door runnels. (David E. Clark)

The final RAF unit based at RAF Morpeth was No.261 Maintenance Unit. It had actually formed at Longbenton in June 1945 as a Ground Equipment Depot within No.56 (Maintenance) Wing and the parent unit had sent an advance party across to the aerodrome earlier that month. The remainder of the unit moved across to Morpeth in September 1945 and the site became a storage area for equipment deemed surplus to requirements. The Maintenance Unit retained a core of RAF personnel but was largely staffed by civilian employees. The runways and taxiways at Morpeth were by that stage closed for flying purposes.

No.261 Maintenance Unit also had sub-sites located at Eshott (until 1948), Holme-on-Spalding Moor, Riccall and Wombleton (all during 1946), and control of the unit passed across to No.55

(Maintenance) Wing on 15th October 1946 when No.56 Wing disbanded. No.261 Maintenance Unit itself finally disbanded on 31st May 1948. By that time, all of the surplus equipment left over from the region's wartime aerodromes had been collected and brought to storage areas such as RAF Morpeth, for scrapping or, where appropriate, to be sold onto private buyers.

Even after the aerodrome officially closed for flying purposes, there were still occasions when aircraft landed on the old runways. According to the accident report, Spitfire Mk.IX EN122, which belonged to No.80 Operational Training Unit at Ouston, had taken off from Morpeth on 3rd January 1946 for a flight back to its home aerodrome. Just prior to landing, the pilot's windscreen iced over, and he could not see properly whilst landing at Ouston. He consequently made a heavy touchdown and the Spitfire's undercarriage collapsed. The aircraft was initially believed to be salvageable but was later re-classified as damaged beyond repair. It is not clear why the Spitfire was visiting Morpeth.

Jack Thompson remembers seeing a Douglas Dakota transport land at Morpeth at some time during the late 1940s, probably in connection with No.261 Maintenance Unit. In addition, de Havilland DH.60G Gipsy Moth G-ABAG force-landed there on 29th July 1950 during the International Air Rally at Woolsington. The turning points for this event were the former aerodrome at Morpeth and the old airship shed at Cramlington. This aircraft is now with the Shuttleworth Trust at Old Warden, Bedfordshire.

One of Jack's lecturers at Durham University, Standish Con O'Grady, used to glide from the former Morpeth aerodrome at weekends at around the same time. The old Newcastle Gliding Club was based there for a while and had at least three gliders available to its members, but the actual types involved are not known.

The Ministry of Agriculture took over the site in March 1951 and the gliding club was forced to move out, relocating to Sutton Bank in North Yorkshire. The government of the day also used parts of the site for storing equipment and Morpeth was "inherited" by the Home Office at some stage during the late 1950s. By this stage, many of the smaller wartime buildings had been demolished or removed. As with many disused sites around the country, some of the hangars at the former aerodrome were used for storage by the Home Office during the 1950s and 1960s. In the case of Morpeth, the large T1 hangars were used to store many of the ubiquitous RAF "Green Goddess" fire engines. These vehicles were kept in reserve at various locations in Britain for use in time of strikes by fire brigades or during national emergencies.

Most of the buildings on the airfield and the surrounding dispersed sites were demolished following the RAF's departure in 1948, and only a few of the hangars, sheds and small huts survived into the 1950s. Virtually all of the structures that survived the initial demolition phase were soon reduced to piles of rubble, including the old watch office.

Go-karting took place on a circuit laid out on the old runways at Morpeth in the late 1950s, although this did not last too long at the site due to the club moving to the eastern end of the main runway at the former RAF Eshott, about seven miles north of Morpeth town centre. The group that operated at the former aerodrome on Wednesday evenings was known as the Swinney Motoring Club.

During the 1960s, there was an incident at the Calder Hall nuclear power station (now known as Sellafield), which was believed to have led to a small release of radiation. Given the prevailing winds over the country, measures were taken to try to detect the spread, direction, and intensity of this radiation. Wartime barrage balloons were brought to Morpeth, inflated, and then tethered with instruments attached to them, these being used to monitor the levels of radiation in the area. Although they were visible from the nearby town, no official explanation appears to have been given to local residents for the balloons being flown from the former aerodrome. The authorities were thought to have even denied their very existence at first. The only trace of their presence at Morpeth are a handful of small concrete cubes which were used to tie down the balloon cables. These have often been mistaken for tie-downs for the aircraft once based at the aerodrome.

Also in the 1960s, a young boy died from drowning at the old RAF sewerage works located just south of Tranwell. Following this incident, the pools that had been left in situ following the closure of the aerodrome were filled in so a similar tragedy could not occur.

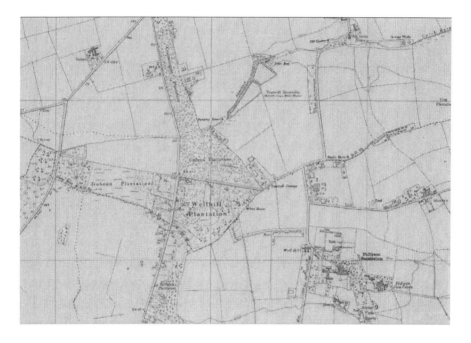

This map from the 1950s shows the remaining buildings that survived on the dispersed sites and also the old aerodrome. Most of the latter had disappeared by the mid-1980s due to a local council decision to clear the site of its dangerous structures. Local farmers who owned the land where the dispersed site lay also took the opportunity to remove these buildings, and only a few isolated ones survived into the 2000s.

In the early 1960s, the former Morpeth aerodrome was allegedly considered as a possible site for Britain's planned intercontinental ballistic missile. This was a land-based forerunner to the eventual submarine-launched missiles that would appear in June 1969, when the Royal Navy assumed responsibility for the UK's strategic nuclear deterrent. If Britain's Blue Streak missile programme had become a reality, then launching silos may have been built at Morpeth, which would also have made the area a prime target for any first-strike Warsaw Pact attack. This would not be the only link with nuclear warheads that the former Morpeth aerodrome would have.

In 1969, a company based in Newcastle tested sections of gas pipeline at the former Morpeth aerodrome site. This process was known as "pre-yielding", and for protection purposes, three sections of earth walls was constructed at the former Runway 17 threshold, adjacent to the Saltwick road on the western side of the old station. These were orientated so that any blast would be directed south-eastwards, i.e. along the open expanse of the old runway and not across the nearby public road. The company also had offices and maintenance facilities located along the western loop, but these were presumably temporary buildings, as there is no trace of their existence.

During the following year, sections of the old runways and taxiways on the southern side of the old aerodrome were dug up to provide hard core for the construction of the A1 Morpeth Bypass, located just over a mile to the north-east. Its proximity to the new road was a bonus for the construction companies involved in the building of the new road, who did not have to bring in material for the foundations from further away.

Air North, the North-East aviation enthusiasts' group, reported that agricultural aircraft from Farm Supply Company were based on the old aerodrome during June 1974, including Cessna 180 Agwagon 230 G-AZZG and Piper PA-25 Pawnee 260 G-BCGO. Presumably the extraction of hard core for the bypass had left enough runway for these machines to safely operate from. Both were engaged in crop-spraying duties and were noted on the old aerodrome again in June 1976. Agwagon G-AZZG was again noted at the aerodrome on 18th July 1977. There appeared to be plenty of work in Northumberland and Durham during the summer of 1976, 1977 and 1978, according to the numbers of aircraft and helicopters engaged in such duties across the region. The contracts would have been seasonal, and therefore these aircraft would not have been based at Morpeth over the winter. Farm Aviation Supply must have been leasing or hiring the Pawnee as it actually belonged to Harvest Air and was usually noted operating from a field near Prudhoe. A second Cessna Agwagon noted at the old Morpeth aerodrome around this time was G-BANI. However, further information - and photographs - on this aspect of the aerodrome's history is rather sketchy.

Light aircraft visitors to Morpeth around this time included Piper PA-28 Cherokee G-ARLK on 22nd May 1975. Noted on 13th and 16th June 1976 was a Jodel DR.1050 light aircraft, G-AYEK, and this also belonged to Farm Aviation Supply. A further light aircraft visitor on 3rd July 1976 was PA-28 Cherokee G-BBLA, one of the Newcastle Aero Club machines. Photographs of these visitors have not been traced, and it may be that none were taken at the time.

One of the T1 hangars was rumoured to have been blown up in a Territorial Army exercise sometime during the 1970s, although a more exact date is unknown. It had apparently been offered to the North East Vintage and Veteran Aircraft Association (later the North East Aircraft Museum), but the fledgling aircraft preservation group could not handle a move of that magnitude. As the Association was formed in 1974, it would seem that the Territorial Army exercise, if it took place, occurred sometime during the mid- to late 1970s.

The Army Air Corps were known to land their helicopters at the former RAF aerodrome on occasions in the 1970s, usually on training flights or cross-country navigation exercises. One such visit involved Westland Scout AH.1 XT553, which turned up on 24th November 1977. The machine also visited the Police Headquarters in Morpeth town centre six days later. The Scout was a small five- or sometimes six-seater light helicopter used for training, liaison and observation purposes, although it did also have a limited attack role, being able to carry a couple of machine-guns on pintles fixed to its skids, and up to four Nord SS.11 anti-tank missiles. Used in Northern Ireland during "the Troubles", a dozen were also sent to the South Atlantic in May 1982 and saw action over the Falkland Islands.

Heavy goods vehicles used sections of the former runways and perimeter track for driver training during the 1970s and 1980s. It seems that half a certain generation of Morpeth residents learned to drive there on an unofficial basis during the same period! Motorcycles were also ridden on parts of the former taxiways, especially the western loop, from the late 1970s until the early

2000s, with hundreds of bikers occasionally turning up on a Sunday to race, show off or just meet up with friends.

Unfortunately, during this time, some riders were seriously injured and one or two were killed. One ended up underneath a car on the nearby road. Needless to say, this could not be allowed to continue, and I noticed that access to the western loop had been finally blocked in early 2002.

According to Hansard, in June 1980, questions were being asked in the House of Commons as to whether *"Saltwick Store on the former Tranwell airfield near Morpeth"* was to be made available for sale or letting on the open market. At that stage, it had not been declared surplus by the Ministry of Defence, who had acquired the land from the Home Office. At the end of March 1990, the Ministry still owned just over two acres of "unused land" at the disused aerodrome, although it is not clear exactly where this was located. It was probably where the small fenced-off compound housing the current telecommunications mast is situated.

There may have been a good reason why the MOD held onto part of the former airfield, even years later when the "Cold War" was rumbling on. Rumours of parts of the old site being used on an occasional basis to park cruise missile convoys persist to this day. According to one post from a local Facebook military history group, fire appliances in support of one such convoy from RAF Molesworth in Cambridgeshire were noticed parked there in December 1986, although the cruise missile transporters themselves were not. It is well known that Albemarle Barracks (the former RAF Ouston aerodrome), near Stamfordham, west of Newcastle, was used to house such convoys on overnight stops as they travelled up and down the country back in the 1980s. Obviously such movements were a matter of national security, wrapped up in absolute secrecy, and casual onlookers would no doubt have received short shrift if they paid more than brief attention to what was happening.

Castle Morpeth Council decided to clear the aerodrome site of most of its surviving buildings in the 1980s, possibly due to safety issues. Most if not all of the structures were considered to be in a poor state of repair and were regarded as a danger to the public.

Motorbikes were ridden in unofficial displays and racing along the former western taxiway loop at Morpeth aerodrome from the 1970s until the turn of the century. By this time, the old airfield site was known to all and sundry as Tranwell. (David E. Clark)

Jack Thompson also saw PA-25-235 Pawnee G-AVXA at Morpeth on 9th June 1984 in addition to a Piper PA-30 Twin Comanche whose identity is unknown. G-AVXA was at that time operated by Agricultural Aerial Services from a farm strip located at Wingate in County Durham. From reports submitted to the *Air North* magazine, it would appear that subsequent years involved helicopters fitted with spray tanks operating from local farms rather than the old

Morpeth aerodrome. One of these was Bell JetRanger G-BBNG, which later operated pleasure flights from Newcastle City Heliport.

In late 2000, former members of Northumbrian Microlights lodged an application with Castle Morpeth Council to operate their microlights from the disused RAF Morpeth site. This followed the group's exit from Eshott aerodrome on safety grounds and also three thwarted attempts to use other locations near the town of Morpeth itself. As was to be expected, given its close proximity, Newcastle International Airport objected to the proposals, as the site was located on the northern fringe of their controlled airspace. After conducting a site visit, Castle Morpeth councillors refused the planning application on local noise pollution grounds.

Despite being closed for flying, Morpeth still provided an aeronautical service into the 21st Century, as it was still used as a Visual Reporting Point for aircraft entering the Newcastle Special Rules Zone. Keith Briggs, an Air Traffic Control Assistant at the airport, recalls that during the 1970s, the Visual Reporting Point was known as "Tranwell", after the nearby village, but this was changed to "Morpeth" by the early 1980s.

The former aerodrome was also deemed suitable as an emergency landing site and was therefore selected as a nominated landing area for locally based light aircraft inbound to Newcastle Airport, should their radios have failed, and if their pilots had been denied entry into the Special Rules Zone for some reason. However, there are no records of it ever being used as such. Even so, it is still believed that the old runways at Morpeth have also used by light aircraft for practice forced landings, although no actual touchdowns took place during these occasions.

A couple of RAF Westland Puma HC.1 troop-carrying helicopters did land at the former aerodrome on the evening of 4th March 1986 during Exercise *Key Lift*. The two machines involved used the call signs *AMG22* and *AMG27*. A few civilian helicopters may have also landed there in the 1990s and 2000s, as they were reported to give "Tranwell" as their destination. However, these may instead have landed in the grounds of nearby private houses, and therefore actual touchdowns on the old aerodrome have not been confirmed.

A model aircraft club operated from the former aerodrome up until the early 2000s, using part of one of the old runways. This group used the site for at least thirty years and apparently had a tenancy "in perpetuity". I witnessed them flying on one Sunday at the end of September 2002, just as I was beginning to believe that they had stopped using the site.

Parts of the old runways and taxiways were definitely used for testing stock cars on occasions. I personally witnessed this on a visit to the site at the beginning of March 2002, when a rather noisy "old banger" was seen hurtling around the old runways at speed.

Car boot sales took place on the former aerodrome up until the start of the Covid pandemic, and the Morpeth Point-to-Point also used the site. The car boot sales, which were held almost every Sunday afternoon during the summer and early autumn for at least two decades, were doing a roaring trade during each year back in the 2000s, the old hangar floors of the two "T1" hangars in the north west corner of the aerodrome providing excellent car parking areas. They restarted in the summer of 2021 before ceasing again for the winter break. I wonder whether the bargain-hunters making use of them realise the history behind the huge concrete expanses?

In October 2009, an organisation known as "Wings Over Northumberland" expressed an intent to develop part of the former aerodrome to *"increase the aviation heritage content of Northumberland"*. Following a two-year-long feasibility study, they had concluded that the site offered an ideal location to establish a new aviation and heritage facility.

The group was looking to re-establish flying at the old aerodrome, initially using the 28-day rule for limited numbers of flight operations. Their aim was listed on their website as follows:

"To create a fully licenced airfield catering for General Aviation types with both grass and tarmac runways, a large heritage contingent comprising of museum and flying historics, and an aerial sight-seeing company."

DISPOSAL OF SURPLUS GOVERNMENT LAND

TRANWELL/SALTWICK NR. MORPETH NORTHUMBERLAND

Re: Hugh Thomas Creighton formerly of North Saltwick Farm, Saltwick, Morpeth, Northumberland.

NOTICE is hereby given that the Secretary of State for Defence wishes to sell the remaining land at the former RAF Tranwell (sometimes known as R.A.F Saltwick) previously owned by Hugh Thomas Creighton formerly of North Saltwick Farm, Morpeth, Northumberland.

Any persons related to, or who have knowledge of the whereabouts of any successor in title to Hugh Thomas Creighton are requested to contact Mr D G Finlay Robinson FSST at the Defence Land Agent, Estate Office, Otterburn Training Area, Otterburn, Newcastle upon Tyne, NE19 1NX by 1 April 1994 at the latest

By early 1994, the Ministry of Defence wished to sell their remaining land at Morpeth aerodrome. This notice appeared in the local newspaper.

A view looking along the western taxiway, taken in March 2002 when access to vehicles had been blocked by the landowner. (Author)

Rather than rebuild one of the old runways, they planned on creating a new grass strip just to the south of the old main one. I knew the two individuals behind the project and was saddened, though not entirely surprised to hear that it never transpired. In addition to the site's proximity to Newcastle International Airport, regular aircraft movements, even general aviation types, may not have gone down too well with residents of the houses that were built in Tranwell Woods in the post-war period. It is a shame that the venture never went ahead at a different location in the county.

Planning permission was sought in 2013 to erect a wind farm on the old RAF Morpeth aerodrome. The developers, Wind Ventures, were looking to install four 126 metre-tall wind turbines at the site. No less than 362 letters of objection were received by Northumberland County Council, including ones from Newcastle International Airport and the Ministry of Defence. Both Mitford and Stannington Parish Councils, plus Morpeth Town Council, also raised their own objections to the plans. Penny Norton, chairman of the Tranwell Windfarm Action Group and Whalton Parish Council, commented on the decision for the local press:

"The action group are delighted as are Whalton Parish and the other councils. We are not against renewables, but they have to be in the right place."

A metal representation of a Spitfire can be found near the gateway of a house not far from the old aerodrome at Morpeth. Whilst this type of aircraft did not serve with No.4 Air Gunners School, the main unit to be based at the station, Spitfires did equip No.80 (French) Operational Training Unit there in 1945. (Author)

In 2016, a half-scale model of a Spitfire and a memorial board were placed outside the St. Mary's Inn near Stannington. These had been created by Charles Lutman, grandson to the man who founded the first model shop in Newcastle. The company supplied balsa wood to the Air Ministry, which used it to build wind tunnel models of aircraft. It was the only memorial connected with RAF Morpeth, as nothing has ever been placed at the actual site of the old station itself. However, by March 2021 both had been removed. The inscription on the memorial read as follows:

"This memorial is dedicated to the airmen of RAF Morpeth.

The airfield initially housed No.4 Air Gunners School (4 AGS). Accommodation was in 10 dispersed sites to the north and east of the airfield near Tranwell village and the Whitehouse Centre (post-war this became a children's hospital). The main aircraft used during its early existence for teaching air gunners was the unpopular Blackburn Botha, which was very heavy and under-powered, often taking the whole of the runway to get airborne. Following several crashes and collisions, it was eventually replaced by the Avro Anson. Most of the air gunnery practice occurred offshore at Druridge Bay, where several of the original wartime structures still exist at the National Trust site and flew between Newbiggin by the Sea and Coquet Island near Amble.

Many of the airmen who flew here were Polish and several settled in the Morpeth area following the war. A large number of Polish casualties including airmen from the airfield are buried in the graveyard of St. Mary's Church, Morpeth.

Other units included No.72 Squadron, RAF, No.80 (French) Operational Training Unit, RAF, No.261 Maintenance Unit, RAF.

No.80 (French) Operational Training Unit was formed in April 1945 at RAF Morpeth to train French fighter pilots using the Supermarine Spitfire and Miles Master.

They shall grow not old, as we that are left grow old,
Age shall not weary them, nor the years condemn.
At the going down of the sun and in the morning,
We will remember them."

When the Inn closed in 2017, Mr. Lutman removed the model and the plaque, and they were apparently stored at his home. A similar Spitfire model, perhaps the same one, was placed at the entrance of a house in Tranwell Woods, less than half-a-mile from the old aerodrome. A new site may well be found for the model, where it can be appreciated without people climbing onto it.

Embraer Tucano T.1 ZF378, which belonged to No.1 Flying Training Squadron based at RAF Linton-on-Ouse in North Yorkshire was painted in camouflage colours in 2017 to celebrate the 100th anniversary of No.72 Squadron. It had been planned to fly the aircraft over the former Morpeth aerodrome on 26th June 2017 as part of a route which involved four Tucanos overflying previous stations used by the squadron. This would have included Ouston, Morpeth and Acklington, but bad weather unfortunately prevented the flight occurring on the day and it never took place.

The former Target Towing Store building was the subject of a planning permission application in 2019, in order to change it into a residential unit. The building and surrounding 0.56 acres of land was valued at a guide price of £150,000. In recent times, the somewhat dilapidated structure was used as a stable, with a static caravan parked nearby for the use of riders. However, work on the building started in the early autumn of 2021.

Across at Druridge Bay, the scene of the air-to-air and air-to-sea gunnery practice sessions, three large concrete structures survive in the sand dunes near the hastily-constructed anti-tank ditch that was incorporated into the area's defences during the war. However, the three buildings are not part of the wartime range. They were built in the post-war period when Druridge Bay was used by No.2 Armaments Practice Station at Acklington and other units that were based there. The larger of the three is the old Main Markers Shelter whilst the other two are Wing Marker observation posts. All three would have had large open observation windows facing seawards but these have all been blocked up to prevent access to the interior of the structures. All may well have been covered in sheet metal to avoid the risk of "friendly fire".

RAF MORPETH TODAY

The western taxiway loop, pictured at the end of March 2021. It bends off to the right in the distance and becomes a narrow, mossy path running through the trees off to the right of shot and back towards the road behind the spot where the photo was taken. The taxiway here is being slowly reclaimed by nature. (Author)

Despite the aerodrome falling into disuse by the end of the 1940s and the destruction of most of the former buildings on the site, there is still a surprising amount of relics to be found. Even though public access is normally limited to a couple of footpaths across the site, car boot sales enabled many more people to visit the old aerodrome, even if they were unaware of the history behind the location. Good views of the former runways and taxiways can be seen from the footpath and the public roads that run along either side of the station. If you use your imagination, your mind can fill in the blanks.

For readers unable to visit the site, or who would like to know what is still visible, here is a description of the aerodrome as it looks at the time of finalising this book (November 2021). Two of the T1 hangars survived into the mid-1970s but have since been dismantled, although the concrete floors still remain as evidence of their former locations and the old door runnels are a bit of a giveaway. The last T1 was removed in 1988 with the intention of erecting it at Newcastle Airport, the other two having already long disappeared by that time.

One of the Miskins Enlarged Over Blister hangars can still be seen on the former aerodrome site, although it seems to have received new corrugated metal cladding over the years. Front and rear corrugated iron walls have certainly been added at some stage, as it was originally open to the elements at both ends. It is not known whether this structure was one of the two that walls were added to during the war, or if this work was carried out afterwards. Otherwise, it was the same building that housed the Blackburn Botha and Avro Anson aircraft during the aerodrome's heyday. Just to the east of this hangar was the site of the Miskins Double Extra Over Blister that was wrecked during the fierce storm in 1944.

One of the former machine-gun ranges stands just to the east of the Saltwick to Mitford road, at the southern end of Saltwick Plantation. The other is located just off a public bridleway running along the southern edge of the former aerodrome. Aircraft would have been parked 100 yards or so from one of these large brick wall-like structures, enabling the turreted machine-guns to be aligned and tested whilst on the ground. The other was used for small-arms practice.

The old Towed Target Store building also survives largely intact and is located on the western side of the site, together with at least one old blast shelter. However, it is currently being converted into "Blackburn House", a private dwelling.

Sections of two of the runways and the northern half of the perimeter track still exist today, along with several "frying pan-type" hard standings. A well-preserved section of taxiway also still exists on the north-western side of the former aerodrome, with road access via the minor road from Gubeon to Ponteland. Most of the latter area is now forested, and a long section of the taxiway is used as a car park when the car boot sales are on.

There are also some surviving building foundations and sections of concrete roadway in Saltwick Plantation, although they are becoming more and more difficult to see due to the undergrowth. Pathways criss-cross this area, used by dog walkers from the new housing estate that now covers the site of the old Mental Hospital.

Quarrying work removed the southern section of the perimeter track over fifty years ago. Mechanical diggers were noted working in this area during January 2002. This was possibly connected with the removal of ash buried there during the early stages of the Foot and Mouth crisis a year earlier. It is believed that around 300 sheep and cattle were slaughtered, burned, and then buried at the site.

The remainder of the aerodrome has been returned to agriculture, mostly grazing land for livestock. With the exception of small areas retained by the Ministry of Supply, all of the land reverted back to private ownership by the 1950s and remains so. As sheep and cattle are farmed on the site, members of the public are not advised or encouraged to trespass. A few areas, especially where buildings once stood, have piles of rubble and other debris, and some of these are covered with a thin layer of moss and vegetation. These can be very dangerous to walk on. Surviving sections of brick and concrete buildings can also be quite unstable, and again pose a hazard to the unwary.

The landowner asks that all visitors to stick to the public footpath that runs across the northern edge of the former aerodrome in order that they can stay safe. This public footpath begins at a stile located at the far north-east corner of the old aerodrome. There are a number of unofficial laybys next to the trees along the Saltwick to Mitford road just south of the path. Most are former entrances to the old technical site, but they have long since been blocked by earthen banks. The path follows the line of the trees bordering the north end of the former flying field, across the foundations of a couple of offices and the Defence Unit's Sergeants' quarters, before passing in front of the surviving Miskin Blister hangar, now used for agricultural storage instead of housing Blackburn Botha aircraft.

Beyond the old blister hangar, the footpath follows the curve of the former eastern taxiway loop before turning north into the trees prior to reaching the northern end of Runway 23. It then joins the north-western perimeter track before turning sharp right along a taxiway which leads to a point between the bases of two of the old T1 hangars. From there, the footpath runs along an old access road to the Gubeon to Ponteland road. The tarmac sections are fine to walk on but the grassy path across to the blister hangar and the one through the trees can be very muddy in wet conditions.

The southernmost gun butts can be found next to a public bridlepath that runs along the southern edge of the old aerodrome. The entrance to this path can be found at a sharp bend on the Tranwell Woods to Saltwick road, about half-a-mile south of the more commonly seen machine gun range. This photograph was taken in September 2021. A taxiway loop just to the north of this structure serviced hangars and parking areas. (Author)

Another public footpath runs along the southern edge of Saltwick Plantation and passes the former machine gun range butts situated just off the Saltwick to Mitford road. The bridleway that begins at a sharp bend about half-a-mile further south along the same road, runs along the southern edge of the old aerodrome site, giving a close view of the second machine-gun butts and leading towards the former RAF Morpeth Battle Headquarters building. These structures were never situated on an aerodrome itself, but instead some distance away so that they would not be immediately overrun by German paratroopers or glider-borne infantry landing on the runways. Battle Headquarters were sometimes converted from existing buildings, although many aerodromes, including Morpeth, had a purpose-built underground structure. Built to Air Ministry drawing number 11008/41, it was a fully-sunken building, complete with thirteen-and-a-half feet thick walls. Nothing short of a direct hit by a large bomb would damage or destroy it. A single staircase led into a passage, off which were a telephone switchboard, a room for messengers and runners (in case the telephone lines were cut) and an office where the defence of the aerodrome would be directed from. There was also an observation post, the top of which just protruded enough above the surface to allow troops to see through a series of narrow viewing slits.

Access to the surviving taxiway loop to the west of the Mitford to Ponteland road has been blocked off by the landowner since the summer of 2002 to prevent vehicular access. A large metal fence still denies entry to the piece of taxiway previously used by youths on motorbikes, while access to the section of the loop further down the road, hidden in the trees, has also been fenced off, although an earthen wall also prevents access by most vehicles. My visit to the aerodrome in March 2002 stirred long-suppressed memories of my father driving me up there from our home in Gosforth in the early 1970s. I can still remember walking around the taxiways where the lorry driving training was being carried out.

Pictured here is a waterlogged blast shelter on the eastern side of the old aerodrome, with the Miskins blister hangar situated at the northern end of the site. Three houses were located just beyond the eastern edge of the flying field, with Greengates actually overlooking station buildings and the airfield itself. This photograph was taken in March 2021. (Author)

What else survives today? Most of the former dispersed sites are located on private land and in any case the buildings that once stood on them have long since been demolished. In fact, unless you know about their locations, it is possible to be completely unaware that anything once stood there.

Instructional Site: Most of the compound has reverted back to agriculture and the remainder is part of a private house's grounds. None of the original buildings have survived.

Communal Site: The most prominent landmark in the area, both in World War Two and today, is the site's old High Level Water Tower, built to drawing number 17286/39. It was capable of holding 60,000 gallons of water. All of the other buildings have disappeared, most of the site reverted to farmland apart from a strip of land adjacent to the Tranwell to Stannington road which is now covered by trees.

Sick Quarters Site: The foundations of the ambulance garage and mortuary building survive in a field adjacent to the Saltwick to Mitford road, but all of the other structures have long since been demolished. The former compound cannot be made out, the site now being part of a farmer's field.

Site 1: All twenty or so buildings have gone, even the old blast shelters. The two former compounds have reverted back to farmland, although aerial imagery shows traces of foundations for the old boundary fence along the southern part of the site.

Site 2: Again, none of the wartime buildings remain here, as farmland occupies the former site. The only evidence is a tarmacadam entrance to a field, which was the entrance to the old compound.

Site 3: The impressions of some hut bases can be made out on aerial imagery but most of the former site is now covered with trees. The western section is now part of the grounds of a private dwelling.

Site 4: No trace of the compound remains. All of the former buildings have been demolished, and the roadways dug up. The entire site is now farmland, and it is even difficult to make out where the old entrance was located.

Site 5: Most of the site has now vanished, apart from a building foundation next to the access road to Site 3, now a farm track. Trees now grow on the northern part of the old compound.

Site 6: The original boundary of this compound can still be made out as a hedgerow, but none of the wartime buildings have survived. It is now a long, narrow grass field.

This old water trough, made by J. Jamieson & Sons of Corbridge, was part of the water supply at RAF Morpeth. It lies among a pile of debris the end of the old Runway 23 and is pictured here in November 2021. (Author)

Site 7: The old 9 foot wide access road still survives but none of the buildings remain standing. Most of the former site has now been covered by woodland.

<u>WAAF Communal Site and Site 1</u>: The access road and former compound now comprise part of Tranwell Farm Camping and Caravan Site. The foundations of the old Dining Room and Institute building survive as impressions and can be easily made out on aerial imagery. However, very few structures survive on this site, the main ones being the central part of the old showers and decontamination block, plus its associated water tower.

<u>WAAF Site 2</u>: All of the buildings have now been demolished. A single structure, a Pump House, survived until at least 2003 but this was knocked down at some stage between then and 2019.

<u>Sewerage Disposal Works Site</u>: Foundations from the old filtration beds survive and can be seen on aerial imagery.

The foundations of some of the technical site buildings in Saltwick Plantation, to the east of the Saltwick to Mitford road, can be seen by simply walking along the lane and looking into the trees. One of the old blast shelters is quite visible but the foundations are more easily seen in winter when the undergrowth dies back. This was the location of the main stores, the parachute store, the main workshops, and the armoury. I spent part of an afternoon exploring this area on a visit in May 2002. When I visited the site one morning in March 2021, shooting was taking place near the old aerodrome site, although it was sporadic and involved shotguns, rather than the staccato sound of 0.303-inch machine guns. However, it was still a poignant reminder of RAF Morpeth's wartime past.

Elsewhere, the remains of a small brick structure can be seen a short way down the northern section of old runway that is used for the car boot sales. From sections of the public footpath through the trees and across one of the old T1 hangar bases, it is occasionally possible to glimpse the Small Arms Store shed to the north, through the trees. It was one of two built. However, this small building lies on the other side of a barbed wire fence and is private property.

The Towed Target Array building located on the western side of the old aerodrome is pictured here in early September 2021. It had been bought with the intention of turning it into a private dwelling. Work had already begun on the conversion when this image was taken, the building's original roof having been removed. It has already been named Blackburn House in reference to the Botha aircraft that served at the airfield in 1942 and 1943. (Author)

EPILOGUE

The wartime water tower at Morpeth is one of the most obvious structures still standing today, largely by virtue of its height and the fact that it can be seen for miles around. The old aerodrome lies about a mile straight ahead. This view was taken in September 2021. (Author)

RAF Morpeth was never a "glamour" station, nor did it house front-line operational units for any appreciable length of time. The airfield has never featured much, if at all, in the memoirs of pilots, in the specialised aviation press or in television documentaries about World War Two. As a training base, however, RAF Morpeth performed admirable service in providing more than four thousand air-gunners for both Bomber and Coastal Commands at a time when they were sorely needed.

Although parts of the former aerodrome have since disappeared forever, and others are fenced off under private ownership, it is still possible to walk along one of the surviving sections of taxiway today and imagine what it was like at RAF Morpeth over seventy-five years ago. Most of the former aerodrome is now private land, having now been returned to farmland or planted with trees. However, those who do not wish to stray far from their vehicle can still see a good view of the former aerodrome from the two minor roads running along the western and eastern sides.

If you pass by the aerodrome at any stage in the future after reading this, take a moment to think what it would have been like to be a young man, maybe hundreds or even thousands of miles from home, in a strange country with a strange language, struggling across a freezing cold aerodrome in a badly fitting uniform and carrying a heavy parachute pack. A clapped out Botha stands before you with a cheesed-off Polish pilot yawning at the controls, someone who really wants to fight the Germans rather than being a glorified taxi driver for some fresh-faced, clueless but snotty air gunner trainees. And then you have to prove you can shoot straight, or at least enough to hit a small cloth and canvas drogue several hundred yards away, without hitting the unfortunate pilot that is towing it. That would have been the experience for many at RAF Morpeth, an aerodrome that should not be forgotten.

ACKNOWLEDGEMENTS

I would like to thank Eric Taylor, Jack Thompson, Keith Briggs and Peter Ure for their help with my research into the three original articles that I wrote about RAF Morpeth back in 2002, which were published in a local aviation enthusiasts magazine. These have been expanded and updated to form the basis of this book. David E. Clark and other members of the Morpeth History Matters Facebook group also provided invaluable assistance whilst I was in the final stages of this project. Christina Spencer graciously allowed me to use her photograph of No.12 Course, the one her grandfather had been a member of back in 1942. Phil Holmes gave up some of his time to show me around part of the land he farms, which once was one of the dispersed sites. Being able to talk to someone who lives and works there really helped give me a different perspective on RAF Morpeth, especially as Phil also shares an interest in what occurred there during the war.

Thanks also go to my long-suffering wife Jo for her support for my writing efforts, and also for accompanying me around a cold and soggy former Morpeth aerodrome in March 2021 so I could update my collection of photographs. She now knows the difference between a T1 shed and a Miskins Double Extra Over Blister hangar!

I have tried to keep errors and typos out of the text but in the end, all mistakes are mine.

APPENDIX 1:
AIRCRAFT BASED AT
RAF MORPETH

Blackburn Botha Mk.I aircraft serving with No.4 Air Gunners School, RAF Morpeth, 1942-1944:

L6115/26 L6116 L6122/28 L6140 L6153 L6161 L6194 L6239/21
L6247* L6275 L6296/55 L6339* L6372 L6374 L6379/27 L6381
L6409 L6441* L6450/17 L6494 L6506/44 L6510 L6513 L6516
L6525 L6531* L6537 L6542 L6544/43 L6546
W5034 W5039 W5043/9 W5044* W5052/18 W5066/2 W5089
W5093 W5096/41 W5107/42 W5112/35 W5119/39 W5120
W5121* W5123/34 W5124/37 W5131 W5133/20 W5134*
W5137/14* W5138 W5139* W5140* W5145 W5146* W5147
W5148 W5149 W5150/6 W5151/7 W5152/8 W5153* W5154/10*
W5155* W5156* W5164* W5165 W5166/58 W5167/29 W5168/30

*Denotes aircraft lost while in service with or on delivery to No.4 Air Gunners School.

Westland Lysander TT Mk.I, TT Mk.III and TT Mk.IIIA aircraft serving with No.4 Air Gunners School, RAF Morpeth, 1942-1943:

L4691 L4693 L4696 L4733 L4736*
R2572 R2575* R2576 R2578 R2581 R2585 R2593 R2597 R2598
 R2621 R2626 R2632 R9070
T1506* T1521 T1560 T1563 T1642 T1671 T1750
V9544 V9681

*Denotes aircraft written off while in service with No.4 Air Gunners School. (All converted from Lysander TT Mk.I, Mk.III and Mk.IIIA aircraft apart from V9681, which was built as a TT Mk.IIIA from the outset.)

Miles Martinet TT Mk.I aircraft serving with No.4 Air Gunners School, RAF Morpeth, 1943-1944:

EM458 EM459
HN864 HN865 HN867 HN881 HN883 HN884 HN885 HN886 HN890
HN891 HN893 HN894 HN907 HN910 HN911 HN912 HN915 HN938
HN939 HN940 HN941* HN965/4 HN966 HN967 HN977 HN978
HP115 HP119 HP128 HP131/21* HP132 HP146 HP170 HP171
HP247 HP253/22 HP254 HP349 HP480/9 HP481* HP513/8
HP514/18
JN430/14 JN431/23 JN432 JN433/30 JN434 JN500 JN601 JN638/19
MS850*

*Denotes aircraft lost whilst in service with No.4 Air Gunners School.

Avro Anson Mk.I aircraft serving with No.4 Air Gunners School, RAF Morpeth, 1943-1944:

N9977
R9709
W2632/I*
AX254
EG691
LT430/K LT487/L LT490/M LT527/W LT720/H LT934 LT935/U
LV132/P LV133/O LV134 LV137 LV145 LV149/T LV160/A LV161/B
LV162 LV163/U* LV164/V LV165/0 LV199/R LV291/C LV292/D
LV297/E LV298/F LV299/G LV300/H LV313/J LV314/P LV315/K
LV316/Q LV317/S LV319/M
MG106/X MG110/L MG111/N* MG241/C MG411 MG415/W
MG512/D

*Denotes aircraft that crashed while in service with No.4 Air Gunners School. Aircraft codes are given where known.

Spitfire Mk.IX aircraft serving with No.80 OTU, RAF Morpeth, April-July 1945:

BR140 BR600 BS247 BS353/3H-E BS403
EN122/3H-H
MA314 MA420 MA422 MA476 MA528 MA593 MA601 MA747
MA818 MH331 MH353/3H-J MH388 MH666 MH876 MH909

Master Mk.II aircraft serving with No.80 (French) Operational Training Unit, RAF Morpeth, April-July 1945:

DK956 DL546 DL892 DM201 DM218

(Not all of the aircraft serving with No.80 Operational Training Unit have been positively identified.)

APPENDIX 2: FLYING UNITS BASED AT RAF MORPETH

No.4 Air Gunners School, April 1942-December 1944
No.72 Squadron, August 1942
No.1614 (Anti-Aircraft Co-operation Flight), April 1943-June 1943
'A' Flight, No.652 Squadron, June 1943
No.80 Operational Training Unit, April 1945-July 1945

APPENDIX 3: AIRCRAFT ACCIDENTS & CRASHES INVOLVING UNITS BASED AT RAF MORPETH

This is not an exhaustive list. Some accidents were not serious enough to warrant the aircraft being withdrawn from use or scrapped. Any damage that could be rectified on site was quickly carried out, whilst more complicated work was completed elsewhere. Most of the aircraft on this list were written off, damaged beyond repair or destroyed in crashes.

17/05/42 L4736 Lysander TT Mk.I - Engine cut; stalled on approach and crash-landed, Morpeth.

24/05/42 W5146 Botha Mk.I - Blown over on take-off, Morpeth.

30/05/42 R2575 Lysander TT Mk.I - Bounced on landing and overturned, Morpeth.

17/06/42 W5153 Botha Mk.I - Force-landed in field after running out of fuel., Benridge Mill Farm, near Mitford.

27/06/42 L4733 Lysander TT Mk.I - Overshot on landing and overturned, blocking road, Morpeth.

06/08/42 BM189 Spitfire Mk.VB - Hit high-tension cables and crashed, Carsphairn; possibly salvaged.

18/08/42 W5155 Botha Mk.I - hit tow rope from T1506, crashed into sea off Amble.

18/08/42 T1506 Lysander Mk.I - tow rope hit by W5155, crash-landed near Amble and burnt out.

19/08/42 W5121 Botha Mk.I - crash-landed at Bedlington after engine failure.

01/10/42 T1521 Lysander TT Mk.I - Crashed on landing at Eshott; aircraft later repaired.

05/12/42 HN941 Martinet TT Mk.I - Force-landed into the sea off Amble after engine failure.

16/11/42 W5139 Botha Mk.I - Took off on wrong runway, collided with L6339, Morpeth.

08/03/43 W5164 Botha Mk.I - Struck tree on take-off and hit trolley, Morpeth.

17/03/43 W5140 Botha Mk.I - Swung on landing; undercarriage collapsed; written off, Morpeth.

29/03/43 W5137 Botha Mk.I - Collided in circuit with W5154, Morpeth.

29/03/43 W5154 Botha Mk.I - Collided in circuit with W5137, Morpeth.

10/05/43 L6531 Botha Mk.I - Flew into hillside, Hazeltonrigg Hill, near Rothbury.

09/06/43 L6441 Botha Mk.I - Crashed on finals, St. Mary's Hospital, Stannington.

22/06/43 W5156 Botha Mk.I - Aborted landing; elevator controls failed; aircraft crashed, Morpeth.

29/06/43 R2598 Lysander TT Mk.I - Engine cut; hit pole in forced landing and undercarriage collapsed, Chevington.

17/07/43 W5044 Botha Mk.I - Struck Anson LV162 while making forced landing at Morpeth.

22/12/43 HP131 Martinet TT Mk.I - Lost propeller and crashed, Morpeth.

01/02/44 ????? Martinet TT Mk.I – force-landed near Amble.

14/03/44 ????? Martinet TT Mk.I - crashed near Acklington.

26/03/44 ????? Martinet TT Mk.I – engine cut on take-off, Morpeth.

30/04/44 ????? Martinet TT Mk.I – crash-landed near Morpeth.

30/04/44 ????? Martinet TT Mk.I – crash-landed near airfield.

01/05/44 HP481 Martinet TT Mk.I - Engine cut; crashed in forced landing, Ulgham.

28/05/44 ????? Martinet TT Mk.I – force-landed about three miles north-east of Morpeth aerodrome.

16/08/44 ????? Martinet TT Mk.I – force-landed one mile north-east of Morpeth on north side of the river.

03/10/44 ????? Martinet TT Mk.I – nosed over on take-off at RAF Morpeth.

06/10/44 W2632 Anson Mk.I - Collided with Anson EF806 and crashed, Higham Dykes.

08/10/44 MS850 Martinet TT Mk.I - Engine cut; belly-landed in field, Warkworth.

All aircraft belonged to No.4 Air Gunners School apart from Spitfire BM189, which was from No.72 Squadron and EF806, the Anson that W2632 collided with, was from No.62 Operational Training Unit based across at Ouston. No records exist for possible losses sustained by No.80 Operational Training Unit.

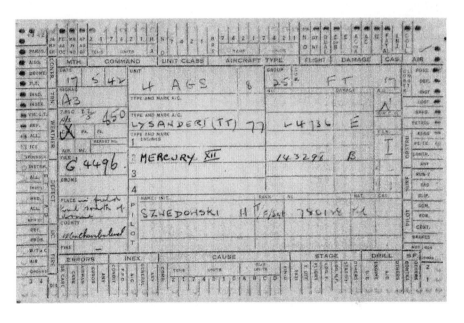

First page of the accident card for Lysander TT Mk.I L4736, which stalled on the approach to Morpeth on 17th May 1942 due to engine failure and crashed ½ mile south of the aerodrome. Details such as the date, unit, aircraft serial number, pilot's name, rank and serial number, the engine type and serial number and the place where the incident happened are all recorded here. The actual locations provided were not always too accurate although in this case it is spot on.

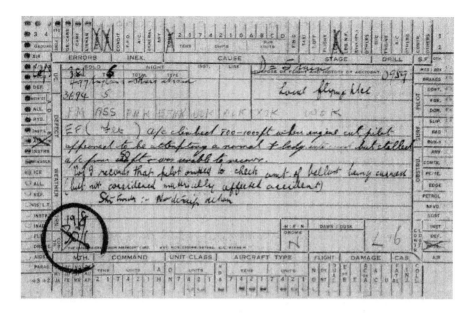

The rear side of the accident card for Lysander L4736 gives a brief indication of the incident and remarks from the investigating officers who looked into the crash. The remarks written on the card read as follows:

"EF [Engine Failure] (Flt) A/c climbed 800-1000 ft when engine cut, pilot appeared to be attempting a normal + lndg [cross landing] into wind but stalled a/c from 50 ft + was unable to recover.

C of I [Court of Inquiry] records that pilot omitted to check amt of coolant being carried (but not considered materially affected accident).

Stn Cmdr [Station Commander]:- No discip action."

APPENDIX 4: PILOTS SERVING WITH No.4 AIR GUNNERS SCHOOL, RAF MORPETH

The following is a list of pilots who are known to have served with No.4 Air Gunners School at RAF Morpeth between 1942 and 1944. Placed in alphabetical, not rank order, it is not an exhaustive list.

Sgt. T. O. Anderson
F/Sgt. Ball
F/Sgt. Barnard
P/O J. Bartelski
Sgt. C. R. Bentley
Sgt. Bisanz
F/Sgt. Burdass
Sgt. B. Carter
P/O W. R. Curry
Sgt. K. M. Davey
F/Lt. J. A. Dziubinski
Sgt. Garstecki
F/Sgt. Gebhard
P/O George
F/O Girard
F/Lt. J. A. Houghton (Flight Commander)
P/O George R. Jackson
Sgt. Jadliszkie
Sgt. Jaworski
Josef Jaworzyn (rank unknown)
P/O W. G. Johnston
Sgt. N. L. Jones
F/Lt. Kaminski
P/O Kay
P/O Kocot

F/Lt. Koniski
F/O E. S. Lavery
Sgt. Lavinston
Sgt. Leech
Medzibrowski (first name & rank unknown)
Sgt. J. Moszoro
Kapral Zgmunt Myszkowski
Sqdn. Ldr. Nicholls
Sgt. Noble
F/Sgt. Oakes
Sgt. Pawlik
F/Sgt. Pearch
Sgt. Proudfoot
Sgt. Radwanski
F/Lt. F. T. Roberts
F/O J. Roberts
P/O Robson
P/O Robinson
P/O Ryszard Reszko
Sgt. Sears
Sgt. Severin
Sgt. W. Shepherd
Sgt. Solecki
F/Sgt. Stabb
F/Sgt. Stewart
Sgt. Switalski
Sgt. Szeckalski
F/Sgt. H. Szwedowski
W/O Szweyowski
F/Lt. T. Symankowicz
F/Sgt. Tatham
F/Sgt. Thomas
P/O Walter Thompson
F/Sgt. E. W. Tranmere
F/Sgt. Walker
Sgt. J. Zalenski

P/O Maciej Zaleski-Slubicz
W/O Zapala
F/Lt. Stanislaw Zarski
Sgt. Stefan Zawilinski
F/Sgt. Zlinicki

SOURCES

AIR 27/578/18 (Record of Events, No.61 Squadron, October 1943
AIR 27/624/71 (Summary of Events, No.72 Squadron, August 1942)
AIR 27/624/72 (Record of Events, No.72 Squadron, August 1942)
AIR 27/1921/15 (Summary of Events, No.463 Squadron, June 1944)
AIR 27/1921/16 (Record of Events, No.463 Squadron, June 1944)
AIR 27/2170/1 (Record of Events, No.652 Squadron, 1942-1944)
AIR 29/590/2, (Operations Record Book, No.4 Air Gunners School, RAF Morpeth)
AIR 50/191/115 (Air Ministry Combat Reports, No.61 Squadron)
Keith Briggs, various emails to the author
Air-Britain, *The Battle File*, 1997
Air-Britain, *RAF Aircraft Serials*, various editions
Air-Britain, *RAF Flying Training & Support Units*, 1997
Air Ministry Form 78 (allocations) for various individual aircraft, RAF Museum
Air Ministry Form 1180 (accident card) for various individual aircraft, RAF Museum
Air North magazine, various issues
Martyn Chorlton, *Airfields of North-East England in the Second World War*, 2005, pg.151-167
David E. Clark, administrator, Morpeth History Matters Facebook group
Peter Clark, *Where the Hills Meet the Sky*, 1997
Commonwealth War Graves Commission Department of Research and Information Services, Royal Air Force Museum, Hendon, London
David W. Earl, *Hell on High Ground Vol.2*, 1999
The *Evening Chronicle* newspaper
Philip Holmes, site visit
The *Morpeth Herald* newspaper
Members of the Morpeth History Matters Facebook group
Newcastle City Library Local Studies Department
R. W. Oxspring, *Spitfire Command*, 1984

David J. Smith, *Britain's Military Airfields 1939-1945*, 1989
Christina Spencer, for permission to use the photo of No.12 Course
Eric Taylor, various letters to the author
Jack Thompson, various letters to the author
Peter Ure, various emails to the author

All of the AIR files bar the No.4 Air Gunners School records were obtained digitally via the National Archives website. AIR 29/590/2 could only be viewed by personally visiting their Kew Gardens site.

ABOUT THE AUTHOR

Graeme Rendall has been interested in Northumberland's aviation past for over forty-five years. A regular contributor of articles to aviation magazines in the 1990s and 2000s, he now writes for *Shadows Of Your Mind* magazine and the American technology and defence website *The Debrief*. He has written five books to date.

Living in rural Northumberland and having recently retired from the National Health Service after 26 years, he enjoys walks in his local area and is now a full-time writer.

ALSO BY THE AUTHOR

The books depicted on the following pages are available via Amazon as either eBook or softback editions:

UFOs Before Roswell: European Foo-Fighters 1940-1945
During World War Two, American and British bomber and night-fighter crews reported seeing strange lights and mysterious objects in the skies over Europe. Officials offered no explanation. They were not Nazi secret weapons, as a thorough search through the ruins of German industry proved after the war. Backed by numerous official reports culled from various archives, this is a thorough examination of the wartime Foo-Fighter phenomenon. 554 pages.

To The Ends of the Earth: A Snapshot of Aviation in North-Eastern Siberia, Summer 1992
The author visited several isolated settlements in the far reaches of north-eastern Siberia, recording the activities of the lifeline Aeroflot services, past and present, plus the local communities. 306 pages.

Northumberland Aviation Stories Volumes One and Two
Collection of tales relating to forgotten aircraft units based in the county, some of the lesser-known crashes that occurred there and plenty of other stories that you may never have heard of.

UFOs BEFORE ROSWELL:
EUROPEAN FOO-FIGHTERS
1940-1945

GRAEME RENDALL
FOREWORD BY SEAN CAHILL

TO THE ENDS OF THE EARTH
A SNAPSHOT OF AVIATION IN
NORTH-EASTERN SIBERIA,
SUMMER 1992
GRAEME RENDALL

NORTHUMBERLAND
AVIATION STORIES

Graeme Rendall

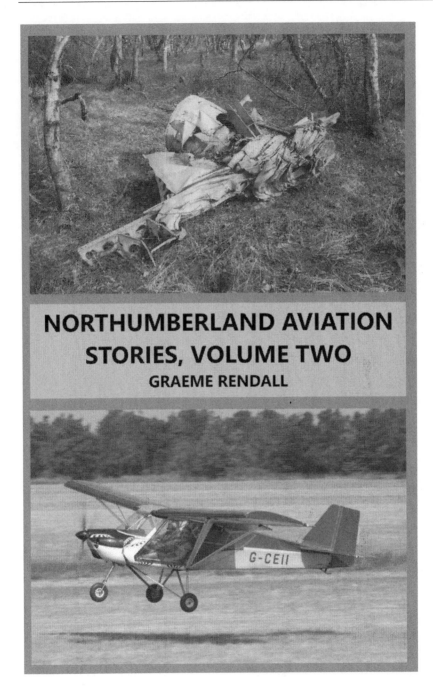

NORTHUMBERLAND AVIATION
STORIES, VOLUME TWO
GRAEME RENDALL

Printed in Great Britain
by Amazon

78749585R00131